PRAISE FOR *SMASH THE*

"Finally—a book that translates the business c... *The Goal* and its ...rful Theory of Constraints into the healthcare setting. Foundational to the science of flow, this is a must-read for anyone engaged in healthcare operations, improvement, and flow. It is impossible to read this book and not have a eureka moment."

Robert Vissers, MD, FACEP, MBA
President and CEO, Boulder Community Health
Adjoint Professor of Emergency Medicine, Faculty Executive Healthcare MBA,
University of Colorado, Denver

"Strear and Sirias address *the* key issue in healthcare operations today—how to break down capacity constraints and realize patient throughput. Full of ready-to-implement examples, their practical application of constraint theory in healthcare will give every hospital director hope that bottlenecks can be smashed and flow restored."

S. Renee Edwards, MD, MBA
Senior Vice President and Chief Medical Officer, OHSU Health

"Strear's and Sirias's *Smash the Bottleneck* is one of the few books on patient flow that guides the reader through this complex process, providing education at a high level without making the uninitiated feel they are overwhelmed by the weeds. The use of the Mattel factory analogy captivates the reader and brings these abstract components to life."

Michael Granovsky, MD
President, LogixHealth

"Using the Theory of Constraints, *Smash the Bottleneck* provides a clear, practical solution to break through the most intractable problem in modern healthcare: patient boarding. This book is a game changer, a must-read for clinical operations leaders in healthcare. Every chapter contains multiple "Aha!" moments. Combining case examples with sound analysis, Strear and Sirias lay out why most patient flow improvement projects predictably fail and how hospital leaders can enable real solutions to improve patient satisfaction, safety, and throughput while improving bottom-line performance."

Ron M. Walls, MD, FAAEM
Neskey Family Professor of Emergency Medicine, Harvard Medical School
Executive Vice President and Chief Operating Officer,
Brigham and Women's Hospital, Boston

SMASH
THE
BOTTLENECK

Christopher Strear
Danilo Sirias

SMASH THE BOTTLENECK

Fixing
Patient Flow
for
Better Care
(and a Better Bottom Line)

ACHE Management Series

Library of Congress Cataloging-in-Publication Data

Names: Strear, Christopher, author. | Sirias, Danilo, 1963– author.
Title: Smash the bottleneck : fixing patient flow for better care (and a better bottom line) /
  Christopher Strear, Danilo Sirias.
Other titles: Management series (Ann Arbor, Mich.)
Description: Chicago, IL : Health Administration Press, [2020] | Series: HAP/ACHE
  management series | Includes bibliographical references and index. | Summary: "This book
  explains how to use the Theory of Constraints to improve patient flow in a hospital, medical
  office, urgent care center, or clinic"—Provided by publisher.
Identifiers: LCCN 2019059855 (print) | LCCN 2019059856 (ebook) | ISBN
  9781640551503 (paperback) (alk. paper) | ISBN 9781640551510 (ebook) | ISBN
  9781640551527 (xml) | ISBN 9781640551534 (mobi) | ISBN 9781640551541 (epub)
Subjects: MESH: Health Facilities—organization & administration | Models, Organizational |
  Efficiency, Organizational | Appointments and Schedules | Patient Care Management |
  Crowding.
Classification: LCC RA971 (print) | LCC RA971 (ebook) | NLM WX 100 |
  DDC 362.1068—dc23
LC record available at https://lccn.loc.gov/2019059855
LC ebook record available at https://lccn.loc.gov/2019059856

The paper used in this publication meets the minimum requirements of American National Standard for Information Sciences—Permanence of Paper for Printed Library Materials, ANSI Z39.48-1984. ⊗™

Acquisitions editor: Jennette McClain; Manuscript editor: Kristen Sweeney; Project manager: Andrew Baumann; Cover designer: Brad Norr; Layout: Integra

Health Administration Press
A division of the Foundation of the American
    College of Healthcare Executives
300 S. Riverside Plaza, Suite 1900
Chicago, IL 60606-6698
(312) 424-2800

To Agnes Kathleen, because writing this book was your idea, and I couldn't have done it without you. Literally.

—Chris

To my beautiful wife, Patricia, and my two outstanding daughters, Denise and Jessica, for being my main source of inspiration.

—Danilo

Contents

Preface

THIS IS DANILO. I want to share a story with you.

A little over two years ago, we first contacted Jennette McClain, an acquisitions editor at Health Administration Press, about publishing a book on the applications of the Theory of Constraints (TOC) in patient flow. She didn't say no, for which we are thankful! As part of that process, we submitted sample chapters and an outline of what eventually became this book. We had a lot of feedback from reviewers—some enthusiastic, some skeptical, and all very enlightening. One reviewer commented that it was interesting to see two professionals from such different backgrounds working together. We thought it was a great story to tell.

In 2014, I was doing a literature review on implementation of TOC in healthcare and found an abstract written by Chris Strear and several other authors. It described the successful implementation of TOC in an emergency department. I used the magic of technology to locate Chris, and thus began a multiyear collaboration. Since then, we have had dozens of conversations that I wish we had recorded. It has not always been an easy collaboration because we are from two different worlds, and at times it seemed like we were speaking different languages. I am a professor of business with a background in industrial engineering, and Chris is a medical doctor with a specialization in emergency medicine. Chris is a practitioner; I am an academic. I live in Michigan; Chris lives in Oregon. I hate needles; Chris is surrounded by them. Our professional language and perspectives are different. However, we share a passion for making healthcare better, and we believe TOC is an essential part of that process.

We continually challenged each other in our conversations, using our expertise to discuss different aspects of healthcare. We looked at multiple healthcare-related case studies around the world to validate some of our assumptions. Some approaches make sense in theory but have no hope of being implemented in practice. Some current practices do not make any sense when viewed through the lens of TOC. Our suggested solutions may be controversial.

A lot of knowledge has accumulated since TOC was introduced, more than 30 years ago, in Eliyahu Goldratt's book *The Goal*. Not all of the tools can be applied at once, so we discussed appropriate implementation sequences. To learn from different industries, we looked closely at implementations in software development and manufacturing. During all this time, we met in person only once. It has been a fascinating journey. At one point, Chris said, "We should write a book." You now have it in your hands.

This book is written from a practitioner's perspective and provides specific strategies to implement TOC in hospitals and clinics. Our objective is to start a conversation about TOC as a methodology that can have a positive impact on healthcare. Feel free to contact us with questions, comments, or suggestions. We hope you enjoy reading the book as much as we enjoyed writing it!

Acknowledgments

DAVID SILVERMAN AND JUSTIN COOK were instrumental in reading and revising our proposal and sample chapters. They helped make the book compelling and readable—and are probably responsible for our editor accepting it for publication. Mike Stone provided a fresh set of eyes when it was time to review our rewrites. All three generously took the time to read additional drafts and refine the book. Justin, a special thank you for fact-checking my Van Halen references (even though they didn't all make the final cut).

In 2007, April Whitworth and Trent Green gave me my first job in patient flow. I would not have had any subsequent opportunities if not for them. They trusted me to do the job—out of faith, desperation, or a little of both. I'm still grateful to this day.

I thought I knew enough about the Theory of Constraints (TOC) to write a book. Then I took a course in constraints management from Russ Johnson, PhD, at Washington State University. Oh, what hubris I had! Dr. Johnson's course was amazing, and this book would not be half as good without his teaching.

My partners in the emergency department at Legacy Emanuel Medical Center picked up considerable slack for me during this endeavor. I had to ditch a lot of shifts toward the end to meet my deadline, and they could not have been more supportive. By stepping in and picking up my shifts, they made this process so much easier for me. I can't tell you how much that meant.

My son, Addison, heard more stories about flow than any 14-year-old should ever have to endure. He was patient through the whole process and made many long weekends of writing more enjoyable.

Finally, I can't say it enough: There wouldn't be a book without Kathy! She never hesitated when I asked her to read chapters (over and over), and each time she reviewed something, she made it much better. Her support kept me focused, and her encouragement kept me going. Thank you.

—Chris

My late mother, Elida, showed me the power of living with purpose. Thank you, Mom, for always believing in me.

I appreciate the many people who helped me, one way or another, in my research journey. All of them were generous in sharing their time and expertise. Dr. Suzanne Savoy initiated me into the healthcare arena and co-authored an early case study with me on the use of TOC in emergency departments. Dr. Gurinder Wadhwa paved the way as one of the pioneers using Lean, Six Sigma, and TOC tools in healthcare; I learned a lot from him. Dr. James Cox's research on scheduling problems in clinics has been valuable to the TOC body of knowledge. His research is rigorous and systematic, and he is passionate about TOC and its implications for healthcare and beyond. His case study in a primary care clinic is included in this book. I had many conversations with Dr. Ruth Vander Stelt about TOC in healthcare, and this book reflects her feedback on my early work using TOC in outpatient clinics. Gijs Andrea, Dr. Roy Stratton, and Bill West were kind enough to receive me and my students in Europe. They gave guest lectures, and they helped organize visits to hospitals in the United Kingdom and the Netherlands so that we could see TOC applications in practice. Bill Taylor showed me the potential of TOC in his groundbreaking work on improving flow in a neonatal intensive care unit. If those babies had been old enough to talk, they would certainly have thanked him. Dr. Gustavo Bacelar and Debashish Naik graciously provided feedback on two of the case studies included in this book that make the theory come to life. Last but not least, thanks to Andrew Kay for our many late-night discussions (for me anyway—in Australia, it was early morning). He has been generous in sharing his expertise and vividly painting his vast experience as a TOC practitioner.

I also want to acknowledge Saginaw Valley State University for its support. Several grants and a sabbatical gave me the time and resources necessary to start my healthcare research. Thanks so much to my tireless research assistant, Louis Pressel, who helped with all my requests.

Finally, none of this could have happened without the work of Eli Goldratt, whom I had the honor of meeting and talking with numerous times on a variety of topics. TOC was his life's work and main contribution to the world.

—Danilo

Thanks to everyone at Health Administration Press for this opportunity. Thank you in particular to Jennette McClain, Andrew Baumann, and Kristen Sweeney for making us sound more eloquent than we actually are and for making this book better than we thought it could be.

—Chris and Danilo

Common Abbreviations

5FS	five focusing steps
APP	advanced practice provider
DBR	Drum Buffer Rope
ED	emergency department
EKG	electrocardiogram
ICU	intensive care unit
MRI	magnetic resonance imaging
MDR	multidisciplinary round
NIOS	nurse-initiated order sets
PCP	primary care provider
PIT	provider-in-triage
TOC	Theory of Constraints
VSM	Value Stream Mapping

Common Abbreviations

Introduction

CHRIS HERE. REMEMBER the TV show *Emergency!*? Before there was a *St. Elsewhere, ER,* or *Grey's Anatomy,* there was *Emergency!* That show was the best! Every week for 52 minutes on NBC, paramedics John Gage and Roy DeSoto got down and dirty in the streets of Los Angeles, saving lives and dishing out excitement as LA County Fire Department Squad 51. The paramedics were the stars of the show, but I couldn't wait until they pulled into Rampart General Hospital to deliver their patients. That's when the magic happened. In the emergency department (ED), Drs. Kelly Brackett and Joe Early stood ready in their long white coats, the picture of competence and authority, to take on whatever came their way. Rampart General! For me, that was as good as it got. That's where I wanted to be.

Cut to 1999. I began my residency training in emergency medicine at Harbor-UCLA Medical Center, a busy county hospital with an amazing staff and some of the sickest patients you could imagine. And guess what—there's a scene in the opening credits of *Emergency!* when Squad 51 pulls into the ambulance bay of Rampart General, lights flashing and sirens blaring, that was filmed at Harbor. My hospital! I was an emergency physician at Rampart General, my childhood fantasy having literally come true!

While the outside of the hospital looked like Rampart, the inside was more like County General from the show *ER.* Our ED was chaotic; people had gunshot wounds and heart attacks, and we raced from patient to patient, trying to keep up. In my three years there, I saw the floors in the waiting room being cleaned only once—there were always too many people to get in there with a mop. During my last year of residency, some of the writers from *ER* came to hang out with us and get story ideas (one of mine even ended up on season four).

We were so busy, and the hospital was so overcrowded, that people might have to wait eight or more hours to get seen. We usually got to the sick patients sooner, but not always. I remember one occasion when a frantic triage nurse called me into the crowded waiting room. People were on their feet, yelling, and the throng of patients had parted to create a path to a young-looking guy, maybe 25 years old, lying motionless on the ground. Another nurse was standing over the man as I reached him, a step ahead of my two co-residents. I felt for a pulse—there wasn't one—and we lifted his body up onto a gurney that had appeared. I hopped onto the gurney and started CPR on the patient as the other residents rushed us back through the waiting room to the ED. We worked on him for another hour, trying to get his heart to start back up. He didn't make it.

I've held a crystal-clear memory of that day ever since. At the time, it seemed like an amazing and heroic effort, riding on top of this dying patient through a crowd of onlookers, pumping on his chest to resuscitate him. It was like a television scene out of *ER*, with me—a younger, better-looking George Clooney—trying to save this guy's life. Now, after decades of experience and perspective, I look back at that day with sadness and regret. This wasn't a patient who died an unpreventable death in his home. He died in our waiting room—our house—with doctors and nurses all around. Our house was too crowded, and we failed him. At the time, we didn't question if we could have done better; it wasn't on our radar then. I had the best medical training available, but I never considered patient flow a necessary part of that training.

Cut to a few years ago. At another hospital several miles from where I now work, a patient walked into the ED waiting room with a head injury. The waiting room was busy. This patient didn't seem to be too sick or in much pain, so he sat down to wait his turn. And then he died. He had an epidural hemorrhage; the blood inside his skull expanded and put too much pressure on his brain. This is a rare occurrence, and it is possible to be fooled by the reassuring appearance of a patient who is, in fact, really sick. However, there should never be a bad outcome because the hospital was too crowded to get to the patient in time. It's unthinkable that someone would come to the hospital with a heart attack and die because we didn't know what to do. Yet we know for a fact that hospital overcrowding can harm patients (as we will soon discuss), so why is it okay that we don't know what to do about poor patient flow? No one should ever be hurt because of overcrowding if the tools exist to manage it. This is why patient flow is important to me, and it's why we wrote this book.

WHY WE NEED ANOTHER BOOK ABOUT PATIENT FLOW

Dozens of books and countless articles have been published on hospital overcrowding and patient flow. Healthcare leaders have been learning about Lean and Six Sigma for decades, and process improvement methodology is part of healthcare master's programs across the country. Despite these efforts, overcrowding remains endemic in healthcare. Poor patient flow is a root cause of overcrowding, so it's not clear how effective those dozens of books and countless articles have been. This book is different. It lays out a methodology that has existed for more than 30 years but has not been widely applied to healthcare—more on this later.

WHY WE SHOULD CARE ABOUT PATIENT FLOW

In 2006, the federal government asked the Institute of Medicine (IOM) to study overcrowding in the emergency medical system. In response, the IOM published three reports describing an overburdened emergency healthcare system that was approaching its limits (IOM 2007a, 2007b, 2007c). In the years since, the situation has only worsened. ED visits have skyrocketed, while the number of available hospital beds has diminished (US Department of Health, Education, and Welfare 1978; Rui and Kang 2014; National Center for Health Statistics 2016).

Hospital overcrowding is important because it has deleterious effects on almost every aspect of healthcare. Hospital overcrowding results in ED overcrowding, which delays treatment for emergency conditions. Patients may take longer to receive pain medication, antibiotics, and imaging studies, and they may have longer hospital stays once they are admitted (Mills et al. 2010; Pines et al. 2010; Singer et al. 2011; George and Evridiki 2015). ED overcrowding also results in more patients leaving the ED against medical advice or without being examined. Consequently, ED overcrowding results in increased morbidity and mortality (Bernstein et al. 2009; George and Evridiki 2015; Singer et al. 2011).

Overcrowding also comes at an enormous financial cost. When a hospital operates at or above capacity, its ED is often forced to close to new ambulance traffic. For every hour that an ED is closed to ambulance traffic, the hospital loses thousands of dollars in potential revenue from ED visits and admissions—ambulances will now take that revenue to another hospital. Hospital overcrowding is frequently caused by stays that exceed the norm for admitted patients as compared to national benchmarks. Most of the hospital's revenue comes from the first few days of a patient's stay. If a patient is benchmarked to stay three days, for example, but is not discharged until the fifth day, the hospital receives relatively little revenue for those last two days of the stay. Although reimbursement for the final two days decreases, the hospital's costs do not. Moreover, the hospital is missing out on the opportunity to put a new patient in the bed and realize higher reimbursements.

The direct financial costs of overcrowding pale in comparison to the indirect costs. Overcrowding poses a significant risk of malpractice, given the higher rates of morbidity and mortality as well as the risks associated with patients leaving against medical advice or before being evaluated. Patients equate long wait times with poor customer service, and bad word of mouth can drive business away.

Hospital overcrowding results in poor patient outcomes, morbidity, and mortality; is a major dissatisfier for both patients and staff; and costs millions of dollars. Overcrowding is bad for business and bad for care.

POOR PATIENT FLOW AND HOSPITAL OVERCROWDING: TWO SIDES OF THE SAME COIN

Patient flow is the most important variable affecting hospital overcrowding. Throughout this book, we use the terms "hospital overcrowding" and "poor patient flow" synonymously. Flow is so vital to patient care that in 2012, the Joint Commission established a patient flow standard (LD.04.03.11), which describes nine performance elements a hospital must meet to ensure compliance. Patient flow is also included in the Centers for Medicare & Medicaid Services quality performance measures. Although healthcare administrators, patient care providers, and hospital staff members understand the importance of patient flow, few healthcare systems have taken significant and enduring steps toward flow optimization.

Hospitals and healthcare systems continue to struggle with patient flow because it's difficult to fix. Improving patient flow requires a wholesale change in staff culture and a clear mandate from the highest levels of administration—not easy to achieve, especially when the mechanics of patient flow are poorly understood.

Overcrowding is typically most visible in the ED, because the ED is the only place in the hospital that cannot close its doors when it gets too full. When other units in the hospital are busy, admitted patients who are waiting for beds on inpatient units back up in the ED. These patients take up bed space in the ED for hours or even days, forcing new ED patients to spill over into hallway gurneys and chairs, or to spend long hours in the waiting room. A stroll through most hospital inpatient wards will show only as many patients as there are available beds, but a casual observer in a busy ED will see patients everywhere: hallways, chairs, and makeshift annexes. Because hospital overcrowding is most visible in the ED, it is often considered the ED's problem to fix. However, as anyone who works in the ED will tell you, ED overcrowding is more often a symptom of a broken hospital system. The entire hospital must therefore be engaged in flow to address ED overcrowding in a meaningful way.

Why is overcrowding such a difficult problem to fix? Many books and conferences offer solutions, but their advice doesn't always translate into successful, actionable, lasting change. Bright, capable people have not been able to definitively solve the overcrowding issue. It might be because we don't know how; or we think we know how, but we don't.

In the past, I worked in a hospital system that was committed to using Lean. Leadership created an entire innovation department, staffed with engineers who were Lean experts. They held educational seminars for hospital employees and scheduled kaizen (improvement) workshops for departments throughout the system. The people who received this training were smart and hardworking, but five years later, there wasn't much to show for their efforts.

The hospital system missed out on opportunities for enduring improvement because it failed to implement effectively. The hospital did not have an overarching strategy, so while the Lean experts skillfully managed individual projects, they were underutilized and deployed randomly. Lean was used for one-off projects based on the biggest fires that had to be put out, which manager hollered the loudest, or who put in a request for resources first. Responding in this fashion rarely yielded long-term, sustainable results. Although the "Lean way" did create some positive gains, its methods were never institutionalized. When the innovation department moved on to other projects, new ways reverted back to old ones.

My medical director at the time experienced the implementation gap first-hand when he was invited to a kaizen on ED flow. My director, Michael Anthony ("Tony" to his friends, and not to be confused with the bassist for Van Halen), trained on the East Coast and brought a blunt, matter-of-fact sensibility with him to the Pacific Northwest. Tony had a finely tuned BS detector, and it started pinging almost immediately on the first day of the kaizen.

Essentially, *kaizen* is a Japanese term for improvement. A kaizen workshop is a Lean tool for continuous improvement. The workshop is typically held over five days and seeks to identify and implement rapid, incremental changes in a specific area of a more complex system. Along with Tony, other participants in the kaizen included the ED nurse manager, the director of emergency and critical care services, the director of social work, the trauma nurse manager, and the Lean expert who was going to help the group "fix" patient flow in the ED.

Unfortunately, the problem with the ED flow had little to do with the ED. The real problem was on the inpatient side, where there were not enough beds to accommodate admitted patients, who then overflowed into the ED. The ED could stop receiving ambulances, but it couldn't close its doors to walk-ins, who made up the majority of ED patients. Tony's ED was overcrowded because the boarded patients left no room for new ED patients. Fixing the ED flow required reengineering inpatient flow, and that was beyond the scope of the kaizen.

My favorite part of this story is when the Lean engineer analyzed the ED using queuing theory and recommended we triple our physician coverage. Tony heard this and apparently went ballistic. He knew that physicians often sat idle because there was nowhere to see new patients. Adding physicians wouldn't create new spaces to see patients; it would only increase provider costs and decrease provider satisfaction.

The group made a few recommendations and implemented them successfully, but the recommendations didn't meaningfully affect overcrowding. As Tony said later, the group nibbled at the edges instead of taking a big bite out of the real problem.

It's all right if a kaizen produces only incremental changes, but the changes need to be embedded in the culture or they will not stick. If positive changes are not institutionalized, people will revert back to their previous way of doing things. Kaizen is a *continuous* process of *ongoing* improvement (much like the Theory of Constraints, as we will discuss throughout this book). It isn't effective to make a change and then stop, move on to something else, and assume any gains made will continue indefinitely.

A one-size-fits-all approach to patient flow typically doesn't work. The causes of poor patient flow differ from hospital to hospital, and solutions also need to be specific to each hospital. People publish books, write articles, and hold conferences touting turnkey solutions to your problems—without knowing what your problems are. What healthcare needs is a methodology for *identifying* specific problems and solutions for individual hospitals. Tackling flow is like the adage "If you give a man a fish, you feed him for a day, but if you teach a man to fish, you feed him for a lifetime." There are many resources that give you a fish, but they don't teach you to fish. Lean, for example, is a popular, thoroughly studied, and widely implemented methodology that has existed for decades. Yet in Japan, the birthplace of Lean and the Toyota Production System, only 20 percent of manufacturers have implemented Lean because it doesn't make sense in every setting (Goldratt 2009). One size does not fit all.

To improve patient flow, you must first understand patient flow. Understanding patient flow requires applying a methodology to your system to identify where it is broken. It's well and good to learn how to set up an observation unit or talk about moving boarders to inpatient hallways (both popular topics in the literature and in flow courses), but these strategies aren't helpful unless observation units and hallway boarders are solutions relevant to your particular problems. To see improvements, you must invest time to understand the problem. Instead of jumping into projects, you must exercise patience.

A good starting point would be a methodology that provides real, lasting change that can be implemented on a manageable scale and expanded as people gain experience with flow.

OUR SOLUTION: THE THEORY OF CONSTRAINTS!

In 1984, Israeli physicist Eliyahu Goldratt wrote a book called *The Goal* (Goldratt and Cox 2016) that introduced the concept of the Theory of Constraints (TOC). Simply put, his theory posits that the productivity of any system is limited at a point in time by a bottleneck resource. Identifying, optimizing, and breaking the bottleneck improves the performance of the entire system.

At this point I want to introduce a concept, then ask you to forget it until much later in the book. This idea is important enough to bring up now but too complicated to discuss thoroughly until we have covered the basics:

> You can maximize a system's performance by using a particular resource, called the *constraining resource*, to synchronize the activity of the entire system—much like a conductor synchronizes the activity of all the musicians in an orchestra.

The constraining resource may or may not be the bottleneck resource. This is a nuanced but important point, and we will return to the constraining resource later in the book. For now, though, we'll concentrate on bottlenecks.

TOC is a process of ongoing improvement, because there will always be a bottleneck in place in any system. Once the bottleneck is broken, another will take its place, which must in turn be identified and broken. *The Goal* was written specifically about a manufacturing plant, but the concepts introduced in the book are widely applicable to all business domains—including healthcare.

I read *The Goal* over a decade ago, and it is no exaggeration to say that the book changed my life! Serendipitously, around the time I completed *The Goal*, I also became the director of our hospital's flow committee. Our hospital was in bad shape—bad enough to make *me* the director of flow. Our inpatient lengths of stay were too long (several patients had been in the hospital for over a year), and our ED was closed to ambulance traffic an average of 60 hours every month. Up to that point, my experience in process improvement had consisted solely of reading *The Goal*, but it was one more book than anyone else had read on flow, so (in my own mind, at least) I was the most qualified to lead our hospital's flow team.

Within months of applying TOC to our hospital's system, we had virtually eliminated ambulance diversion. Our rates of ED patients who left without being seen fell sharply, and our inpatient length of stay dropped to levels below the national benchmark. We accomplished these achievements during a devastating influenza season and a period of record ED patient volumes, ambulance traffic, and patient admissions. We no longer had to close to ambulance traffic, which put less pressure on the EDs at other hospitals. Our efforts helped reduce the diversion rates at almost every other hospital in the region. Our department became so productive that we were able to add full-time ED nursing positions for the first time in years. Even though we were busier, the work felt much easier. Staff members were happier, employee retention was at an all-time high, and we improved the hospital's bottom line by several million dollars in the first year alone. Most important, we sustained the improvements for years. Since that time, we have introduced TOC to many of our other hospitals.

A QUICK WORD ABOUT LEAN AND SIX SIGMA

Lean and Six Sigma are additional methodologies used to improve operations throughout a system. Similar to TOC, they both have their origins in manufacturing but have been applied widely to the healthcare sector. Each has its own unique strengths and challenges, and both share some similarities with TOC. Lean and Six Sigma are both better-known entities in the healthcare domain, perhaps owing to earlier adoption or first-mover advantage—or maybe they had better publicists.

Each methodology can be characterized in the simplest terms as follows.

TOC:	Focus
Lean:	Waste
Six Sigma:	Variability

Each methodology can offer improvements if implemented correctly. More recently, however, practitioners have found tremendous operational advantages from combining all three methodologies. This makes sense, as one method can act synergistically with the others.

For example, Lean emphasizes waste elimination and empowerment of frontline workers, making it a powerful tool for gaining efficiencies, leveraging insights, and increasing employee participation. However, the emphasis on waste elimination may make a system anemic, with too much focus on cost reduction and not enough on increased output. Moreover, Lean does not offer an obvious starting point for system-wide flow improvement; there is no prioritization in the search for waste. Lean does not emphasize synchronization of resources across a system, nor does it necessarily break down silos.

Six Sigma seeks to reduce variability in a system, thereby reducing defects and bad outcomes. Although Six Sigma's emphasis on quality can result in better products or improved outcomes, it may result in only modest improvements to patient flow. Six Sigma also lacks a clear prioritization mechanism.

One of the greatest advantages of TOC is that it looks at the entire system and answers two key questions: "Where do we start?" and "Which resource should we concentrate on?" With its emphasis on focus, TOC makes it easier to determine how and where to get started and, hence, gets faster results!

Synthesizing the three methodologies offers the greatest advantage to hospital systems. We recommend first using TOC to observe the system and determine where to begin and on which critical resource to focus. Once TOC has answered these questions, you can incorporate properties of Lean (eliminating waste, but only as it affects the bottleneck) and Six Sigma (primarily to reduce variability in usage of the bottleneck resource) to realize maximum gains in efficiency.

USING THIS BOOK

The purpose of this book is to teach you how to use TOC to improve flow in your hospital, medical office, urgent care center, or clinic, but anyone committed to improving patient flow and decreasing hospital overcrowding should also read *The Goal*: It has been part of the core curriculum in business schools and corporate offices for 30 years. The book you are currently reading outlines the principles described in *The Goal* and applies those principles to healthcare. We discuss

- how TOC differs from Lean;
- how to identify bottlenecks in your own hospitals and clinics; and
- how to exploit and break bottlenecks, improve patient flow, enhance care, and strengthen the bottom line.

Throughout the book, we use common bottlenecks to illustrate certain concepts. Although these examples may not be the bottlenecks in your organization, the methodology still applies to your system. Finally, we explore constraint management (remember that thing I told you to forget?) through use cases—specifically involving ED flow, inpatient flow, and outpatient settings— to illustrate fully synchronized systems. As you read through each chapter, we encourage you to think about how the principles discussed relate to your hospital or clinic setting.

SUMMARY

- Hospital overcrowding has detrimental effects on both the cost and quality of patient care.
- Overcrowding is endemic in our healthcare delivery system.
- Methodologies exist to improve flow, but they are often applied incorrectly or incompletely and have not always been particularly effective.

- Three of the most well-established methodologies are TOC, Lean, and Six Sigma.
- The emphasis of TOC is focus, the emphasis of Lean is waste, and the emphasis of Six Sigma is variability.
- Aspects of each methodology can be combined to achieve synergistic improvements in patient flow.

REFERENCES

Bernstein, S. L., D. Aronsky, R. Duseja, S. Epstein, D. Handel, U. Hwang, M. McCarthy, K. J. McConnell, J. M. Pines, N. Rathley, R. Schafermeyer, F. Zwemer, M. Schull, B. R. Asplin, Society for Academic Emergency Medicine, and Emergency Department Crowding Task Force. 2009. "The Effect of Emergency Department Crowding on Clinically Oriented Outcomes." *Academic Emergency Medicine* 16 (1): 1–10.

George, F., and K. Evridiki. 2015. "The Effect of Emergency Department Crowding on Patient Outcomes." *Health Science Journal* 9 (16): 1–6.

Goldratt, E. M. 2009. "Standing on the Shoulders of Giants: Production Concepts Versus Production Applications. The Hitachi Tool Engineering Example." *Gestão & Produção*. Published July/August. www.scielo.br/scielo.php?script=sci_arttext&pid=S0104-530X2009000300002.

Goldratt, E. M., and J. Cox. 2016. *The Goal: A Process of Ongoing Improvement*. New York: Routledge.

Institute of Medicine (IOM). 2007a. *Emergency Care for Children: Growing Pains*. Washington, DC: National Academies Press.

———. 2007b. *Emergency Medical Services: At the Crossroads*. Washington, DC: National Academies Press.

———. 2007c. *Hospital-Based Emergency Care: At the Breaking Point*. Washington, DC: National Academies Press.

Mills, A. M., B. M. Baumann, E. H. Chen, K. Y. Zhang, L. J. Glaspey, J. E. Hollander, and J. M. Pines. 2010. "The Impact of Crowding on Time Until Abdominal CT Interpretation in Emergency Department Patients with Acute Abdominal Pain." *Postgraduate Medicine* 122 (1): 75–81.

National Center for Health Statistics. 2016. "Hospitals, Beds, and Occupancy Rates, by Type of Ownership and Size of Hospital: United States, Selected Years 1975–2014." Table 89 in *Health, United States, 2016*. Accessed November 14, 2019. www.cdc.gov/nchs/data/hus/2016/089.pdf.

Pines, J. M., F. S. Shofer, J. A. Isserman, S. B. Abbuhl, and A. M. Mills. 2010. "The Effect of Emergency Department Crowding on Analgesia in Patients with Back Pain in Two Hospitals." *Academic Emergency Medicine* 17 (3): 276–83.

Rui, P., and K. Kang. 2014. "National Hospital Ambulatory Medical Care Survey: 2014 Emergency Department Summary Tables." Centers for Disease Control and Prevention. Accessed November 14, 2019. www.cdc.gov/nchs/data/nhamcs/web_tables/2014_ed_web_tables.pdf.

Singer, A. J., H. C. Thode, P. Viccellio, and J. M. Pines. 2011. "The Association Between Length of Emergency Department Boarding and Mortality." *Academic Emergency Medicine* 18 (12): 1324–29.

US Department of Health, Education, and Welfare (DHEW). 1978. *Health, United States, 1976–1977.* DHEW Publication No. (HRA) 77-1232. Accessed December 17, 2019. www.cdc.gov/nchs/data/hus/hus7677.pdf.

PART I

Smashing the Bottleneck: Moving Patients Through the Hospital

TOC IS A PROCESS of continuous improvement that can be applied to any system to enhance flow. TOC was introduced by Israeli physicist Eliyahu Goldratt in his seminal 1984 business novel, *The Goal*. Its methodology has been adopted by *Fortune* 500 companies worldwide and is a standard part of business school curricula. TOC has its roots in manufacturing but is applicable to virtually any industry. It is used to improve flow by identifying and coordinating all the activities in a system around the single critical resource that most constrains the system's productivity. This single-minded focus distinguishes TOC from other operational methodologies, such as Lean and Six Sigma, making TOC easier to implement and improvements easier to obtain and maintain. As we will discuss later in the book, combining all three methodologies creates a synergistic effect that helps maximize flow through the critical resource once that resource has been identified.

TOC has only recently started to gain traction in healthcare delivery. In *The Goal*, Goldratt introduces a process of ongoing improvement that uses five focusing steps (5FS) to manage the critical resource of a system. The guiding principle is that improving flow through the critical resource, or bottleneck, will improve flow through the entire system.

In the following chapters, you will learn how to apply the 5FS to a healthcare system, identify and exploit the critical resource, and then break the bottleneck.

While the bottleneck may differ from one hospital or clinic to another and solutions to break the bottleneck may be unique to any one healthcare system, the way you apply the methodology—how you use TOC to identify constraints and solutions—is universal.

CHAPTER 1

Understanding the Fundamentals of the Theory of Constraints

OBJECTIVES

- Define precise operational measurements for evaluating productivity under TOC
- Define productivity measurements in the context of a healthcare system
- Explain bottlenecks
- Introduce the five focusing steps for the process of ongoing improvement

---

WHEN I (CHRIS) was in the fifth grade, our teacher gave us a six-page test and told us it was timed. As soon as she said go, I tore through the pages, determined to finish first. The test consisted of a series of questions and tasks: "Draw three triangles inside three circles." "When red and blue are mixed together, what color do they make?" The questions weren't difficult. Halfway through the test, the instructions said to speak your name out loud. I was the first in the class to reach this point. Three pages later, I was a few items away from finishing. I was sure I was ahead of everyone else. I looked up at my best friend Brad, who was sitting at his desk—hands folded in front of him, pencil off to the side. What the heck? But I was too close to being first to worry about Brad. Toward the bottom of the last page, I read: "Say 'I'm almost done' out loud." Again, I was the first in the class to do so. The second-to-last item read: "Don't complete any items except for the first and the last." The final item: "Sit quietly with your hands folded in front of you and your pencil off to the side." I nervously went back to item number one, which I now realized said: "Read all items first before starting." Forty years later, I can still see Brad looking at me and smiling, and I can still feel my face turning red.

My takeaway from that experience was: Next time, cheat off Brad. Another, more enduring takeaway is that it is important to think through any strategy completely and critically before jumping in. Doing so will save a lot of time (and maybe some embarrassment). It would be great to know if an idea that was *meant* to improve patient flow actually *would* improve patient flow before committing time and resources to it. You have probably worked on a committee that successfully executed a project everyone assumed would help improve flow, only to find that after countless meetings and hours of implementation, the project didn't move the needle. A project can be completed without being effective. In *The Goal*, Eliyahu Goldratt refers to this as a "nonproductive move." It is important to determine whether a project will be productive or nonproductive prior to getting started.

TOC uses three measurements to predict whether a project will be productive or nonproductive: throughput, inventory, and operating expense (exhibit 1.1). While these measurements may seem simple and intuitive, their definitions are precise:

- *Throughput* is the rate at which the system generates money through sales.
- *Inventory* is all the money the system invests in purchasing things that it intends to sell.
- *Operating expense* is all the money the system spends to turn inventory into throughput.

These measurements can be applied to virtually any system where materials move through a stepwise process to a finished product—for example, a widget factory that starts with raw materials, alters these raw materials through a series of steps,

Exhibit 1.1: The Three Operational Measurements of TOC

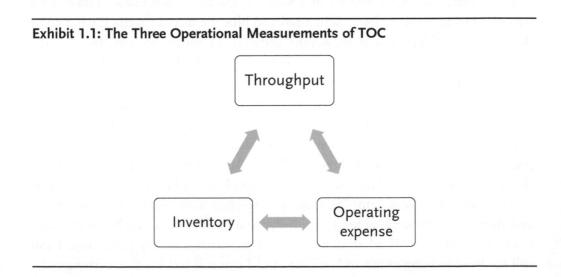

Exhibit 1.2: Effect of a Productive Move on Operational Measurements

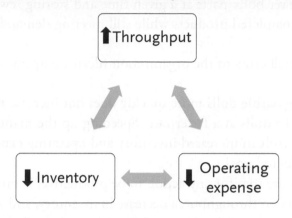

and ultimately makes a finished widget. The materials and product can be broadly defined and are relevant to systems outside of the manufacturing sector.[1]

For a move to be productive, it should increase throughput while simultaneously decreasing inventory and operating expense (exhibit 1.2). At the very least, any move must affect two of these measurements while holding the third static.

Consider, for example, a Mattel factory that manufactures Barbie dolls. Inside the factory, raw materials are combined and processed through a series of steps to create a finished product. For simplicity, assume that each Barbie doll is made by combining six parts: head, body, two arms, and two legs. These individual body parts constitute the raw materials.

The throughput is the rate at which the individual body parts (the raw materials) are combined into a completed Barbie doll and the doll is packaged and sold for money. The inventory is the money the company spends to purchase body parts. Inventory also includes the finished dolls that have not yet been sold as well as partially completed dolls that are somewhere on the assembly line (also known as works-in-process). Operating expense is the money used to turn the body parts into the completed Barbie doll as well as the costs associated with storing, selling, and shipping the completed product and any other costs associated with turning raw materials into finished dolls.

Any business decision Mattel makes regarding Barbie doll production is potentially disruptive and costly, but it may also reap huge rewards for the company. The managers at Mattel can use operational measurements to predict whether a business decision is likely to be productive or nonproductive. For any change in operations to be productive (i.e., make more money), that change must simultaneously result in the following outcomes:

- Making and selling Barbie dolls more quickly (increase throughput)
- Purchasing fewer body parts at a given time and storing fewer works-in-process and completed products while still meeting demand (decrease inventory)
- Reducing overall costs to the organization (decrease operating expense)

Note that making Barbie dolls more quickly does not increase throughput unless Mattel also sells the dolls at a faster rate. Speeding up the manufacturing process in isolation may result in increased inventory and operating expense, which is the opposite of the desired goal.

It bears repeating that for any action to be productive, it must simultaneously result in an increase in throughput, a decrease in inventory, and a decrease in operating expense. However, of the three variables, throughput is the most important. If all you do is increase throughput, the entire system still benefits. Customers receive more products and services, the company improves its finances, and employees have more stability. Throughput is so important that an action can be productive even if it increases operating expense, as long as it increases throughput by a higher amount.

OPERATIONAL MEASUREMENTS IN HEALTHCARE

How do these operational measurements apply to patients in a hospital setting? If you consider each patient as analogous to a product, you can see how TOC is used in patient care. In a factory, a product starts with parts or materials that go through a stepwise process to be altered or assembled into a finished product, which is then sold. Throughput measures how quickly this process occurs. Inventory is the money tied up in raw materials, works-in-process, and unsold finished product. Operating expense is the money it costs to turn inventory into finished product (including the cost of storing the parts and unfinished products until they are sold).

In healthcare, a patient starts with a symptom, abnormal test result, or health concern and must go through a stepwise process to be diagnosed, treated, and discharged. In the healthcare setting, the measurements of throughput, inventory, and operating expense apply directly to patient flow through a hospital, clinic, or office-based practice in the following context:

- *Throughput* is the rate at which a patient moves through a hospital, clinic, or office-based practice.[2]
- *Inventory* is the number of patients at different stages in the hospital, clinic, or office-based practice.

- *Operating expense* is all the resources used in evaluating, diagnosing, treating, and discharging patients, plus all the other costs associated with running the hospital, clinic, or office-based practice.

Throughput can be measured for an entire hospital or for one specific area or unit. For example, ED throughput is measured from the time a patient registers in the ED to the time the patient is discharged, admitted and transferred to an inpatient unit, or transferred out of the ED to another hospital. Inpatient throughput is measured from the time a patient arrives at a unit (e.g., medical-surgical, telemetry, critical care) to the time the patient leaves the unit (e.g., transfers out of the intensive care unit [ICU], is discharged from the hospital ward). Throughput can also apply to a patient's entire hospital length of stay, from the time the patient first registers to the time the patient has physically left the hospital. To improve throughput, you must change the process for evaluating, diagnosing, treating, and discharging patients.

Since throughput is the rate at which the hospital generates money through sales, it must include the entire time a patient is physically in a hospital bed, even if the patient's discharge order has been written (patients are considered inventory until they no longer physically occupy their hospital beds, just as a widget is considered inventory until it is actually sold and moved out of the factory). Examples include an ED patient who is being admitted but is boarding in the ED or an inpatient who has been discharged but is still in the hospital room waiting for a ride home. Patients boarding in the ED are one of the biggest indicators of poor flow in a hospital and are often a starting point for identifying bottlenecks.

Similar to throughput, inventory can be measured by patient census over the entire hospital or in a specific department or unit. Examples of inventory include the number of patients in the ED, ICU, or operating suites. Inventory can also be defined as a subset of patients in a department, such as patients in the ED waiting room who have yet to be evaluated or admitted patients who are boarding in the ED. Inventory can even consist of patients awaiting treatment who are not in the hospital but may be waiting at home for a procedure or clinic appointment.

Operating expense refers to the money spent to run the hospital: salaries for physicians, nurses, technicians, and housekeepers; utility bills; hospital supplies; food; and linen costs. Essentially, operating expense includes all the money that the hospital spends to treat patients. Operating expense also includes money that the hospital spends independent of patient census: upkeep on imaging equipment, for example, or licensing fees. The hospital incurs these expenses even if it has no patients to treat.

As in manufacturing, the goal in healthcare flow is to increase throughput, decrease inventory, and decrease operating expense. For a hospital, this means faster dispositions (the rate at which patients are evaluated, treated, and discharged), decreased time that a patient stays in the hospital (shorter lengths of stay, fewer avoidable days), and more efficient treatment plans (judicious use of laboratory and imaging studies, standardized supply chain, implementation of evidence-based protocols).

We can illustrate the power of TOC operational measurements by applying its basic principles to a case study (adapted from Han et al. 2007).

CASE STUDY

An urban, academic Level 1 trauma center with 45,000 annual visits underwent a major expansion to increase the size of its ED from 28 to 53 licensed beds. The expectation was that the expansion would cause ambulance diversion times to decrease, but when the hospital studied the effects of the expansion on ED flow, it found no significant change in ambulance diversion times, the number of episodes of ambulance diversion, or the duration of each episode. Moreover, both the total ED length of stay and the length of stay for boarded patients in the ED increased after the expansion.

What happened?

Let's answer the question of what happened in terms of our three operational measurements: throughput, inventory, and operating expense. To be a productive move, doubling the number of ED beds would need to increase throughput, decrease inventory, and decrease operating expense. What effect did the expansion have on each measurement?

The hospital believed it could accommodate more emergency patients by doubling its number of ED beds. Does this move improve throughput? Remember that throughput is the rate at which a patient moves *through* a department, not just into a department. The hospital made no changes to its process of evaluating, treating, or discharging patients and, therefore, has not improved throughput. Some patients will now wait to be evaluated, treated, and discharged in a bed instead of the waiting room, but whatever factors previously limited patient flow are still in effect. The new beds will soon be filled with additional patients who are parked in the ED. Doubling the number of ED beds makes the parking lot bigger, but it doesn't move cars out of the lot faster.

What effect does the expansion have on inventory? If the rate at which patients leave the ED is unchanged, then inventory will probably not go down.

The number of patients in the waiting room may decrease initially, but an equivalent number of patients will be parked in the newly built ED beds. The ED has become a bigger parking lot, and inventory will soon increase.

How does this move affect operating expense? Operating expense will increase; the additional beds will require more staff to maintain nursing ratios, more work for housekeeping, more supplies to stock the new rooms, and more utility costs. A bigger parking lot is more expensive.

Building more beds in the ED without improving the process of diagnosing, treating, and discharging patients either will not affect throughput or will decrease it somewhat (due to added inefficiencies that result from boarding more patients). An expansion will increase inventory and operating expense. It is a nonproductive move.

Hopefully, it now seems obvious that the plan in the case study was doomed to fail. After reading only a few pages, you have become more skilled in patient flow than the hospital leaders who approved the ED expansion. TOC has provided insight that could have saved tens of millions of dollars on an expansion that did not achieve the hospital's goals. You have learned that before starting a project, you must first ask if the project will be productive, and you have started to learn how to answer that question. Operational measurements seem intuitive and simple to understand, but they are both powerful and often ignored.

To summarize:

- Any move that increases throughput, decreases inventory, and decreases operating expense is productive, and any move away from this goal is nonproductive.
- Throughput is the most important of the three measurements.
- The operational measurements must be applied to all potential projects before beginning any project.
- A project can be successfully executed, but that doesn't mean it will be productive.

Our objective, then, is to find actions that are productive.

UNDERSTAND THE BOTTLENECKS

A bottleneck is any resource whose capacity is equal to or less than the demand placed on it. Every system has (at least) one main bottleneck that limits the rate of output for the entire system. It is often the most critical resource of the process, and its capacity may not be easily increased. Bottlenecks can occur due to a temporary situation, such as an unexpected increase in demand, a machine breaking down, or a key person being absent from work. Bottlenecks may also be self-inflicted, the result of practices and policies such as batching work (e.g., doing all elective surgeries on Mondays) or excessive multitasking.

The key to TOC is to identify the scarcest resource in a supply or service chain and improve the use of that resource, thereby improving flow through the entire system. Let's create a hypothetical scenario for our Barbie doll example to illustrate a bottleneck. Assume that Mattel needs a million pieces of each of the six body parts to meet its production target. It has one million pieces for five of the parts, but only one thousand pieces of the right arm. In this example, the right arm is the bottleneck.

A nonbottleneck is any resource whose capacity is greater than the demand placed on it. All of the body parts other than the right arm are nonbottleneck resources. Since there is a shortage of right arms, there are more of the other body parts than the factory can use at the present time.

A bottleneck resource's productivity determines the productivity of the entire system. Bottlenecks are important because Mattel can produce only as many Barbie dolls in an hour as there are right arms available. If the factory has the capacity to produce one million dolls in an hour but has only one thousand right arms (the bottleneck) available in that hour, then the entire factory can make only one thousand dolls.

An hour lost on the bottleneck is an hour lost for the entire system. Once the bottleneck resource is used up (no more right arms), the factory sits idle. It can't produce any more finished products without additional right arms.

The cost of an hour lost on the bottleneck is the cost of an hour for the entire system. While the factory sits idle, waiting for more right arms to be delivered, it is not producing finished products and, therefore, is not generating revenue. However, the factory's fixed costs do not change, and it continues to incur expenses roughly equal to the expenses it incurs when it is producing goods to sell.

An hour saved on a nonbottleneck is a mirage that does not affect productivity. Let's say that at the Mattel factory, there are six teams of workers and that each team is responsible for one of the body parts. The factory manager may notice the right-arm team sitting idle while the factory waits for a shipment of right arms. The manager transfers the right-arm team members to the other teams, believing that the plant's efficiency can be improved by eliminating downtime. Now each of the five other teams is faster at assembling its respective part—but this action has not saved the factory any time because the entire factory is waiting on the avail-ability of right arms to complete the product. This move has allowed the factory to make one-armed Barbie dolls more quickly, but since Mattel can't sell one-armed Barbies, throughput (the rate at which Mattel makes money through Barbie sales) is not affected, and time is not actually saved. Moreover, the manager's decision has driven up inventory (as there are now 999,000 one-armed Barbies piled up behind the right-arm station) and increased operating expense (since Mattel now has to pay to store the unfinished products). Mattel did not make additional money despite improving the speed of the nonbottleneck teams by keeping all the workers busy.

Saving time on a nonbottleneck introduces the concept of *local optima*. In a system where departments operate as silos, a change made in one department may seem to improve efficiency but only if productivity is measured for that specific department. When you look at the overall picture, the change may prove non-productive (e.g., making 999,000 one-armed Barbies). Further, local optimization may reduce throughput through the entire system, increase inventories and operating expense, and move the system away from productivity. If saving time on nonbottlenecks increases inventory, increases operating expense, and makes the plant more chaotic (by creating more works-in-process and piles of inventory), the organization has moved away from its goal.

FIVE FOCUSING STEPS

Process improvement requires identifying a system's bottleneck resource and then breaking it. In *The Goal*, Goldratt outlines five steps, called focusing steps, used to identify and break the bottleneck. Note that every system has a bottleneck; bottle-necks are neither good nor bad—they are simply an inherent part of any process. Once one bottleneck has been broken, another will appear. For this reason, TOC is a process of *ongoing* improvement.

The 5FS that comprise the foundation of TOC are:

Step 1: Identify the system's bottleneck.
Step 2: Decide how to exploit the system's bottleneck.
Step 3: Subordinate everything else to the decision made in Step 2.
Step 4: Elevate the system's bottleneck.
Step 5: If the bottleneck has been broken, go back to Step 1.

Step 1 is to identify the bottleneck. You do that by looking for a pileup of inven-tory in the system; the bottleneck will most likely be the resource in front of the highest pileup. In Step 2, you decide how to exploit the bottleneck. This means developing the necessary strategies to keep the bottleneck resource up and running every hour of every day. Remember that an hour lost on the bottle-neck is an hour lost for the entire system. Step 2 of the 5FS is the heart of the

TOC operational strategy. Deciding how to exploit the system's bottleneck will determine how the rest of the resources are managed. You execute Step 3 by deciding how your other resources will support the activities designed in Step 2. Step 3 requires you to prioritize the constant production of the bottleneck above all other activities—including subordinating personal agendas and institutional methodologies. In this step, you identify and reengineer local policies to benefit your system as a whole. This involves breaking down silos and changing culture, making it the most involved and meatiest of the five steps. Step 4 is to elevate the bottleneck: If, after exploiting the bottleneck resource, there is still need for greater capacity, you may need to invest in additional quantities of the bottleneck resource or in other resources that can augment the bottleneck. Finally, once you have broken the bottleneck, you return to Step 1 and look for the new bottleneck in your system. Without the vigilance of Step 5, the system will revert back to its original state and you will lose any gains made from the 5FS.

Let's apply the 5FS to our Mattel factory.

Step 1: Notice the pileup of left-armed Barbie dolls. The inventory pileup sits behind the bottleneck resource—the right arm.

Step 2: Decide the right-arm assembly station should never sit idle: There should never be any down time at this station.

Step 3: Subordinate all other factory workflow to the decision made in Step 2. Reorganize the workflow so that the right arm is assembled first. The right arm assembly will never have to wait on the other body parts (the nonbottlenecks) to be assembled. As soon as another right arm becomes available, make sure it gets attached to a Barbie. When no more right arms are available, stop assembly until you obtain more right arms. This avoids pileups of works-in-process.

Step 4: Increase capacity of the bottleneck. Find other factories that can supply right arms; salvage right arms from other, unsold types of Barbie dolls (e.g., Lawyer Barbies and Rock Star Barbies); purchase extra left arms and turn the hands around; buy surplus G.I. Joe right arms and come out with a special edition Barbie with Kung-Fu Grip.

Step 5: Recognize when right arms are no longer the bottleneck, and go back to Step 1 to find the new bottleneck.

Now that we have introduced the 5FS, we can discuss how to apply them to healthcare.

SUMMARY

- TOC is a process of continuous improvement to optimize flow through a system.
- Throughput, inventory, and operating expense are operational measurements used to determine if a change in the process will be productive or nonproductive.
- Throughput is the rate at which the system generates money through sales; inventory is all the money the system invests in purchasing things it intends to sell; and operating expense is all the money the system spends to turn inventory into throughput.
- The goal of TOC is to increase throughput, decrease inventory, and decrease operating expense.
- In a healthcare system, throughput is the rate at which a patient moves through a hospital or clinic; inventory is the number of patients at different stages in the hospital or clinic; operating expense is the cost of evaluating, diagnosing, treating, and discharging patients, plus all other costs associated with running the hospital or clinic.
- The goals in a healthcare system are faster dispositions, decreased time that a patient stays in the hospital or clinic, and more efficient treatment plans.
- A bottleneck resource is any resource whose capacity is equal to or less than the demand placed on it.
- TOC uses the 5FS to identify the bottleneck and improve flow through the bottleneck:
    - Step 1: Identify the system's bottleneck.
    - Step 2: Decide how to exploit the system's bottleneck.
    - Step 3: Subordinate everything else to the decision made in Step 2.
    - Step 4: Elevate the system's bottleneck.
    - Step 5: If the bottleneck has been broken, go back to Step 1.

NOTES

1. A note about these measurements: Throughput is technically the price paid for a product, less the variable costs that specifically depend on how much it costs to produce an additional unit—raw materials, for example. Fixed costs such as labor or rent fall under the category of operating expense. The throughput is expressed as a rate $/unit of time, where $ refers to margin made from sales and time refers to the period of time being examined. Additionally, as the practice of TOC matured, inventory became known as investment and included all assets that could be sold (e.g., equipment, buildings). Here again, we will focus on inventory as defined in the text.

2. We'll leave out the part about the product being sold as a part of throughput (remember, it's a rate at which the system generates money). Strictly speaking, throughput involves the money the healthcare system generates by treating patients, which is largely dependent on reimbursement by commercial payers or government payers. Practically speaking, flow in healthcare is not dependent on reimbursement, so in these discussions, throughput will simply be the rate at which a patient moves through the system.

REFERENCE

Han, J. H., Z. Chuan, D. J. France, S. Zhong, I. Jones, A. B. Storrow, and D. Aronsky. 2007. "The Effect of Emergency Department Expansion on Emergency Department Overcrowding." *Academic Emergency Medicine* 14 (4): 338–43.

CHAPTER 2

The First Focusing Step:
Identify the Bottleneck

OBJECTIVES

- Learn how to identify the bottleneck
- Test your hypothesis about the bottleneck

I (CHRIS) DRIVE my kids to school, and on the way, there is a stretch of road under construction. Traffic backs up as three lanes merge into two, and then into a single lane. It can take over 20 minutes to move four blocks. I like to use this time to impart wisdom to my children and wax eloquently about flow—if I listen hard enough, I can actually hear their eyes rolling. Undaunted, I explain how we in the cars are inventory piling up behind the bottleneck—an available lane—and I remind my children how lucky they are to have a father who is so wise and generous with his knowledge. At this point, my teenager in the front seat looks at me, sighs loudly, and turns up the radio; there we all sit, piled up behind the bottleneck, waiting to merge.[1]

To identify a bottleneck, look for the biggest pileup of inventory: The bottleneck will be the resource in front of the pileup. In a hospital setting, inventory can refer to patients in a specific part of the hospital, such as patients in the ED or the ICU, or it can comprise all of the hospital's patients. If there is a pileup of patients waiting to be seen by a physician in the ED, then the bottleneck may be physician staffing. If there is a pileup of patients who have been medically cleared and are waiting to be discharged from an inpatient service, then the bottleneck may be a lack of skilled nursing or assisted living facilities to accept patients upon discharge.

In the initial stages of process improvement, the biggest bottleneck will likely be obvious. In fact, the biggest pileup will probably be an issue that everyone has been complaining about for years, and the bottleneck will be sitting right in front of that pile.

Whether obvious or not, it is helpful to go through the formal process of identifying the bottleneck. This ensures that all stakeholders working to improve flow agree on the bottleneck. It is also good practice for subsequent iterations of the 5FS, in which new bottlenecks may be less obvious.

The easiest way to identify a bottleneck is to build a process map of patient flow through the entire hospital system (exhibit 2.1). This basic, high-level map provides a good starting point for identifying the bottleneck. Note that analysis should be done during typical patterns of flow and not in extreme or unusual situations where an unexpected event is causing excessive delays. Use exhibit 2.1 to find the bottleneck by looking for a pileup of inventory: Where is the patient census higher than it should be?

Waiting Room

Is there a pileup of patients in the waiting room? There is no set number of patients that defines a pileup other than some quantitative number of patients that everyone decides is too many. It can be a function of a high rate of patients who leave without being seen or a prolonged "door to bed" or "door to provider" time that signifies excessive wait times. If there is rarely a pileup of patients in the waiting room, the bottleneck is likely external to the system—a function of the marketplace. Under those circumstances, the hospital has the capacity to treat more patients in its ED without stressing the system and should focus on growing patient volumes.

Exhibit 2.1: Process Map of Hospital Patient Flow

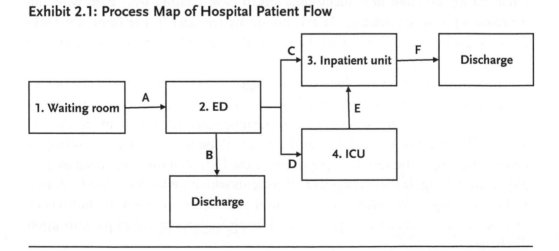

Emergency Department

If there is a pileup of patients in the waiting room, is there also a pileup of patients in the ED? A pileup in the ED occurs when all ED beds are full and there is no availability to move patients out of the waiting room. Visual cues of an ED pileup include inpatient boarders taking up ED beds and gurneys occupied by ED patients lining the hallways. Additionally, the ED length of stay for admitted or discharged patients may be too long and ambulance diversion rates too high (recall that ambulance diversion is usually symptomatic of a broken hospital system rather than indicative of an ED-specific problem).

If there is not a pileup of ED inventory, then the bottleneck exists at arrow A in exhibit 2.1—the outflow of patients from the waiting room to the ED. Causes could include inefficient registration or triaging processes, as well as delays in rooming patients such as when a charge nurse purposely leaves ED beds empty. A more granular process map is then made to focus on the specific steps at A, and that map is used in subsequent focusing steps. If, however, there are plenty of open, staffed beds in the ED, then a project designed to discharge patients from the ED more quickly will likely have no significant effect on overall flow. This is an example of how an hour saved on a nonbottleneck is a mirage.

If there is a pileup of ED inventory, then you need to discover whether ED lengths of stay are long for discharged patients, boarders, or both. There may be a pileup of ED patients who will ultimately be discharged from the ED or an accumulation of admitted patients (boarders) waiting for a hospital bed in either an inpatient unit or the ICU (or both).

If the ED pileup consists of discharged patients, then the bottleneck resource exists at B in exhibit 2.1, and the hospital should focus on the process of evaluating, treating, and discharging patients from the ED. It would be useful to create a more detailed process map tracking a patient's movement from the time the patient reaches the ED up to and including discharge. If patients are also backing up from the ED into the waiting room, it may be helpful to include the waiting room in the process map, even though the bottleneck may not exist in the waiting room. Reorganizing workflow in the waiting room may be an important strategy to break the ED bottleneck in subsequent focusing steps.

Inpatient Units

If there is a pileup of ED boarders waiting to move to an inpatient unit, is there also a pileup of inventory on the inpatient units? The hospital needs to identify whether, for example, all of the inpatient beds in a unit are full or whether there are empty beds that are staffed, clean, and ready to accept patients. The hospital should also determine whether its average inpatient length of stay (when adjusted for acuity) is longer than published benchmarks.

If there is not a pileup on the inpatient units, then the bottleneck exists at C in exhibit 2.1. Subsequent focus should be on the process of moving patients from the ED to inpatient units, including how beds are ordered and assigned, how physician handoff is conducted, how nursing reports are given, and how patients are transported to the accepting unit.

If there is a pileup of inpatients, are they predominantly patients who are medically ready to leave the hospital (i.e., patients for whom a discharge order has or can be written)? If the answer is yes, it indicates a delay, either in writing the discharge order or in the patient physically leaving the hospital despite being discharged. If patients are waiting for the treating physician to write a discharge order, then the delay exists upstream of the discharge order, and the physician may need to start his or her day earlier or round on potential discharges first. If, on the other hand, patients have discharge orders but are unable to leave the hospital—for example, they are waiting for family members to pick them up or for a room at a rehab or skilled nursing facility to become available—then the delay exists downstream of the discharge order. In either scenario, the bottleneck exists at F in exhibit 2.1.

If the pileup is not the result of delays before or after discharge orders have been written, then the focus of improvement must include the time during which the patient is actively receiving treatment and has not yet been cleared for discharge. Are inpatient lengths of stay longer than published benchmarks suggest they should be? Benchmarks allow a hospital to compare its own length of stay to standards based on the performances of other hospitals (adjusted for patient volumes and acuity). If patients are not medically cleared for discharge within the expected time frame, then subsequent strategies must address patient care from the time patients are admitted until the time they receive discharge orders. Questions to ask during this part of the process can include: Are patients typically responding to treatment as expected and ready for discharge within that predicted time frame, or are they staying longer than expected? Are patients receive imaging studies, social work evaluations, physical therapy, and medication teaching in a timely fashion? Are nosocomial infections or iatrogenic complications keeping patients in the hospital longer than anticipated?

Intensive Care Unit

If there is a pileup of ED boarders waiting to move to the ICU, is there also a pileup of patients in the ICU? In other words, look to see whether ICU beds are always full. If there is not a pileup of ICU patients, then the bottleneck exists at D in exhibit 2.1, and the process for improvement is analogous to examining C.

If there is a pileup of ICU patients, it is possible that all of the patients need ICU-level care. If so, the hospital should examine how its ICU lengths of stay compare to published benchmarks, similar to the inpatient exercise above. If lengths of stay are longer than expected, subsequent strategies should focus on patient care delivery while in the ICU and similar questions asked about patient response to therapy, timely ancillary services (e.g., labs, imaging), and nosocomial infections. If lengths of stay in the ICU are not longer than expected, it may be that the ICU does not have enough beds and the hospital needs to add capacity (this focusing step, elevating the bottleneck, is discussed in subsequent chapters).

On the other hand, the pileup may be the result of patients boarding in the ICU while waiting for an available inpatient (non-ICU) bed. If inpatient beds are available, the bottleneck exists at E in exhibit 2.1. If inpatient beds are not available, the next steps are analogous to those laid out earlier for inpatient units. In the event of competition for an inpatient bed between an ICU patient ready to transfer out and an ED boarder, the available bed should usually go to the ICU patient first (assuming that the ICU is full—otherwise, there is no urgency to transfer the ICU patient out).

In Short . . .

In short, look for a configuration where a significant number of patients are waiting on a unit followed by a relatively small number of patients waiting on the subsequent unit. Such a scenario indicates the likely location of the current bottleneck.

WHERE DO WE GO FROM HERE?

After you have identified the bottleneck, try creating a process map that details patient flow on either side of the bottleneck. If the bottleneck resource is in the ED, for example, create a detailed process map of the components of patient flow leading into and out of the ED (i.e., patients in the waiting room trying to get into the ED and patients in the ED trying to leave the ED). Exhibit 2.2 presents a more granular process map of patient flow through the ED.

While exhibit 2.1 provided a useful starting point for identifying the bottleneck, exhibit 2.2 provides the necessary detail to identify the bottleneck itself.

CONFIRM YOUR BOTTLENECK: THE SNIFF TEST

After you have identified a potential bottleneck, test that hypothesis by envisioning how the system would change if the bottleneck had unlimited capacity. If the hypothesized bottleneck was ED physician staffing, for example, and the imagined system now has ten times the number of ED physicians working

Exhibit 2.2: Detailed Process Map of Patient Flow Through Emergency Department

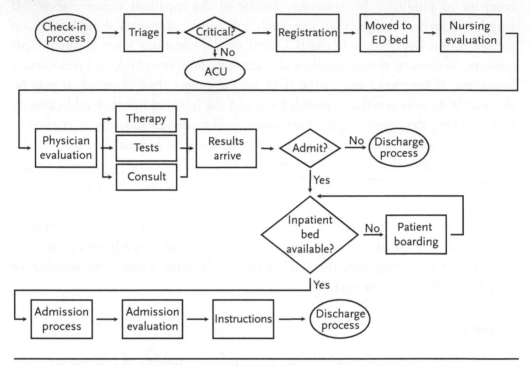

at any given time, determine whether flow would improve dramatically for the whole system. (Practically speaking, we recognize that adding unlimited capacity is probably not feasible and could actually make the problem worse by increasing inventory.) If the hypothesized move helps significantly, and if it creates a new bottleneck in the system, you have probably correctly identified the bottleneck.

Let's apply what we have learned to a case study.

CASE STUDY

A Level 1 trauma center averaged 60 hours of ambulance diversion each month. The CEO estimated that every hour of ambulance diversion cost the hospital $10,000, generated bad publicity, and denied services to the local community. The hospital applied TOC to identify the bottleneck in its system: For a month, whenever the ED went on ambulance diversion, the charge nurse recorded the reason (exhibit 2.3).

Based on this data, where is the hospital's bottleneck?

(continued)

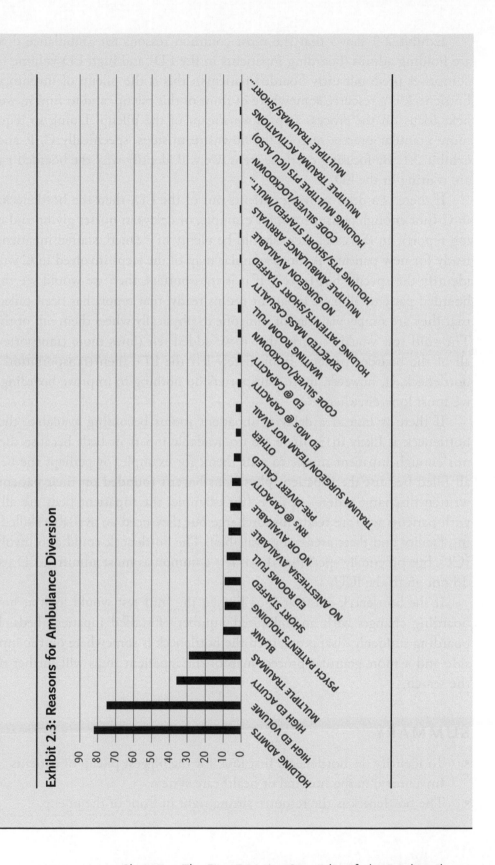

Exhibit 2.3: Reasons for Ambulance Diversion

Exhibit 2.3 shows that the most common reasons for ambulance diversion are holding admits (boarding inpatients in the ED) and high ED volume (which comprises predominantly boarded patients); this is the pileup of inventory. The bottleneck is a resource somewhere in front of this pileup, and to find it, we must next focus on the process steps downstream of the pileup. Doing so requires a more granular process map of the downstream steps, specifically C, F, and 3 in exhibit 2.1. By focusing on these steps, we will identify why the boarded patients are waiting in the ED.

If there is a delay moving patients out of the ED, then the bottleneck exists in C (not enough transporters, for example, or delays in nurses giving and receiving report). In this case, there should be plenty of cleaned, staffed inpatient beds ready for new patients. A more granular map of the steps involved in C will help identify the specific bottleneck. If it is transporters, then we would see that the boarded patients all have inpatient rooms ready, that report has been called, and that they are simply waiting for someone to physically wheel them out of the ED. The sniff test would confirm that if we added ten times more transporters and all of the boarded patients immediately left the ED, then transportation is the bottleneck. If, however, more transporters do nothing to improve boarding, then we must look elsewhere.

If there is instead a delay in inpatient rooms becoming available, then the bottleneck is likely in 3 (there are no available inpatient beds because there are not enough inpatient nurses to staff them, for example, or perhaps the beds are all filled because the inpatient physicians haven't rounded on their patients and written discharge orders) or in F (for example, the inpatient beds are all filled with patients who are ready for discharge but they need an available skilled nursing facility and there aren't any available). The bottleneck could also involve the ICU, but practically speaking, this is less common as most admitted ED patients do not go to the ICU.

If the bottleneck exists at 3 or F, then the sniff test would look at how ED boarding changes with an unlimited number of staffed inpatient beds. If ED boarding suddenly disappears, then the bottleneck is somewhere on the inpatient side and a more granular process map of the inpatient steps will further narrow the search.

SUMMARY

- To identify the bottleneck, first look for the biggest pileup of patients (inventory) in the hospital or healthcare system.
- The bottleneck is the resource sitting right in front of the pileup.

- After identifying the bottleneck, create a granular process map of the steps adjacent to the bottleneck—those that flow into or feed the bottleneck and those that flow immediately away from or out of the bottleneck.
- Teenagers don't appreciate how wise we are.

NOTE

1. Incidentally, you know how there always seem to be construction workers at these sites walking around with hardhats and orange vests, but it's not clear what exactly they are doing? They could be considered nonbottleneck resources! I suspect that if you added more of these construction workers, we'd still be sitting in traffic just as long; remember that an hour saved on a nonbottleneck resource is a mirage.

CHAPTER 3

The Second Focusing Step:
Exploit the Bottleneck

OBJECTIVES

- Understand what it means to exploit the bottleneck
- Understand how to exploit the bottleneck

EXPLOITING THE BOTTLENECK means never having any idle time on the bottleneck. In other words, you want to use the bottleneck resource as much as possible. By definition, demand on the bottleneck already exceeds its current capacity; if the bottleneck sits idle, the demand-capacity mismatch is made even worse.

Drinking Fountain

Remember when you were a kid on the playground at recess and had just finished a hard-fought game of tag? You raced to the only working drinking fountain on the playground and stood behind a line of parched second-graders, waiting your turn. Remember how annoying it was when the kid at the front of the line took a drink and then stood there while he swallowed, wiped his mouth, looked around, took a swig and spit it out, then wiped his mouth again? While precious seconds ticked away, the bottleneck resource (the fountain) sat idle. No one else could drink from the fountain while the kid at the front of the line was standing there. The longer the fountain sat with nobody actually drinking from it—in other words, the longer kids stood there monopolizing the resource—the more kids went thirsty. There's no way to make up for idle time on the bottleneck—you can never get it back. The schoolyard teacher wasn't about to lengthen recess so everyone could get a drink.

Let's revisit a few key points about bottlenecks:

- An hour lost on the bottleneck is an hour lost on the entire system. In our example, the system is children waiting for a drink during recess. Since the end of recess is a hard stop (i.e., bottleneck capacity is limited), when the fountain is idle, the entire system goes without water.
- What the bottleneck produces in an hour is what the system produces in an hour. The number of kids who get a drink from the fountain dictates the amount of the system that gets water.
- An hour saved on a nonbottleneck is a mirage that does not affect productivity. The students could line up more quickly, but if the fountain isn't running, they still aren't drinking any faster.

To exploit the bottleneck, you need to keep the fountain running the entire time that kids are lined up for a drink. In fact, to truly exploit the bottleneck you would need to have someone drinking from the fountain during the entire recess.

A Return to the Mattel Factory

Let's now return to the Mattel factory producing Barbie dolls to see how we can exploit the bottleneck in this system. We identified the bottleneck in production at the right-arm station. To exploit the bottleneck and eliminate idle time, we need to determine if there is idle time at this station. If so, we need to understand which specific step(s) in the process generates idle time. We need to break down this part of the process into more granular steps; hone our focus from the system as a whole to the bottleneck resource; and drill down to the steps that immediately feed the bottleneck, the steps that use or incorporate the bottleneck, and the steps that immediately follow the bottleneck. Our analysis will highlight times when the bottleneck is not being actively used (i.e., when the right-arm station sits idle).

We need to create a more detailed map of the process immediately before, during, and after the bottleneck to determine if there is idle time during these steps. Incidentally, creating a detailed process map is similar to the concept of a gemba walk in Lean, where walking the shop floor is essential to understanding the process and eliminating waste. In TOC, we also seek to eliminate waste, but in this case we define waste specifically as idle time on the bottleneck rather than

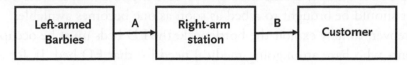

idle time in the entire system. (Idle time on the nonbottlenecks is acceptable as long as the bottleneck does not sit idle. In fact, you want some idle time on the nonbottlenecks, or you risk turning a nonbottleneck into a new bottleneck—but more on that later.)

A more detailed process map of the Barbie doll assembly would have three steps. In exhibit 3.1, a left-armed Barbie comes to the right-arm station via a conveyer belt (arrow A). Workers pick up the doll and attach a right arm (right-arm station). The completed Barbie is then placed back on the conveyer belt to head toward the next station (B), where it is then shipped to the customer.

Exhibit 3.1 helps us identify several times when the bottleneck could sit idle. Upstream of the bottleneck, there could be a delay in getting left-armed Barbies to the right-arm station; this would cause the right-arm team to sit idle while waiting for product even if they had right arms available. There could be downtime within the right-arm station: The workers at this station could all get a break at the same time, or the conveyor belt could be stopped for maintenance every day during peak production time. The problem could also be downstream of the bottleneck (B in exhibit 3.1); if a downstream bottleneck caused production to back up (e.g., if finished dolls aren't being shipped to customers on time and the warehouse is full), there would not physically be any room at the right-arm station for workers to affix additional right arms. After breaking down the key processes around the bottleneck, we would next want to interview managers and assembly-line workers, review performance data, and walk the shop floor to find out why there is downtime on the bottleneck.

EXPLOITING THE BOTTLENECK IN A HOSPITAL SYSTEM

Emergency Department Bed as Bottleneck Resource

In a hospital system, suppose that the bottleneck is an empty bed in the ED. In this scenario, the ED waiting room is filled with patients who are piled up, waiting for an available ED bed. If there are empty beds ready for new patients but the beds aren't being filled, then those empty beds are not being exploited. Every minute a bed sits empty is idle time on the bottleneck. To exploit the bottleneck, a patient should be brought to a bed as soon as one becomes available.

Moreover, to fully exploit the bottleneck, the ED beds must be occupied only by patients who have an ongoing medical need for that ED bed. If, for example, ED beds are occupied by patients who are ready to leave but are waiting for discharge orders, then the bottleneck is not being exploited.

To explore how we might exploit the bottleneck (in this case, an available ED bed), we must create a more detailed process map that focuses on the bottleneck resource. Exhibit 3.2 is based on the high-level process map from exhibit 2.1. In our example, the bottleneck resource is an ED bed that exists in the box labeled "ED" in exhibit 3.2. That means we would find a pileup of patients in the waiting room—since the bottleneck has a pileup of inventory sitting behind it—but there would be available beds in the inpatient units and ICUs.

If there was instead a pileup of inventory in the waiting room but an excess of beds in the ED, then the bottleneck would be a resource in the waiting room (a triage nurse, for example) or in the process of moving patients from the waiting room to the ED (arrow A in exhibit 3.2).

If there was also a pileup of patients on the inpatient units and that pileup backed up into the ED, then we would find the bottleneck somewhere within or somewhere downstream of the inpatient unit (e.g., F).

Returning to our example of the ED bed as bottleneck resource, we must next create an even more granular process map for the steps immediately upstream of the ED (A), within the ED itself, and the steps immediately downstream of the ED (B, C, and D). In this way, we focus on processes that feed into the

---

Exhibit 3.2: Process Map of Patient Flow in the ED

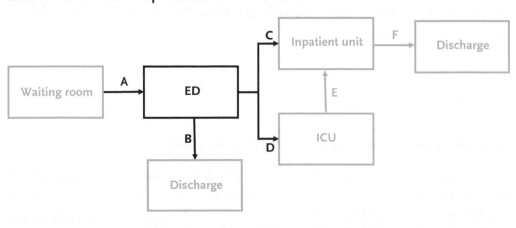

---

bottleneck, the bottleneck itself, and processes that empty out the bottleneck. The more granular map not only helps identify times when the bottleneck sits idle but also illuminates where we should start looking to make changes in workflow to enable us to exploit the bottlencck (this is the third focusing step and will be discussed in the next chapter). Items to note on a walk-through of the ED would include empty gurneys or beds ready and waiting for patients; dirty beds that need to be cleaned; and patients who are ready for discharge occupying beds. Such circumstances create idle time on the bottleneck; to exploit the bottleneck, this idle time must be identified and eliminated. Any idle time can be traced to the bottleneck itself or the activities immediately upstream and downstream of the bottleneck.

To understand how the ED bottleneck is affected by what happens in the waiting room (the upstream processes that feed the bottleneck), we need a granular process map of the activities at arrow A in exhibit 3.2. In exhibit 3.3, we see that the charge nurse identifies the next appropriate waiting room patient to be brought back to the next available ED bed; the charge nurse then communicates with the triage nurse, who brings the patient back to the open ED bed.

In examining the activities in exhibit 3.3 (i.e., "walking the shop floor"), we may find that various factors contribute to downtime on the bottleneck. The charge nurse may have too much responsibility, causing a delay in matching an open room to a waiting-room patient or in communicating with the triage

Exhibit 3.3: Granular Process Map of Patient Flow Upstream of the Bottleneck

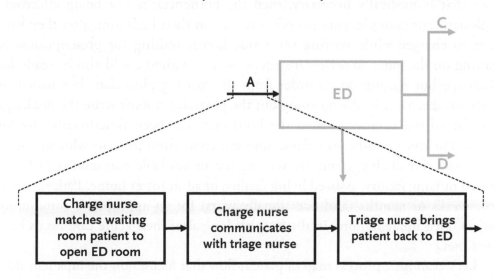

nurse. The triage nurse may be too busy to speak with the charge nurse or to find waiting-room patients and escort them back to the ED. The patient may be in the bathroom or outside when his or her name is called, or may have left altogether without being seen. Any one of these delays results in an available ED bed sitting empty—in other words, idle time on the bottleneck.

To fully identify processes that are inefficient and may contribute to idle time on the bottleneck, we must also create more granular process maps for B, C, and D. These detailed maps will typically reveal redundant or unnecessary steps, or processes with too much variability that introduce inefficiencies into the system (a classic focus of Six Sigma). In all cases, we must identify and minimize or eliminate actions that contribute to idle time on the bottleneck.

Inpatient Bed as Bottleneck Resource

Let's now consider the inpatient units. It is common for a hospital's inpatient beds to be full, with patients boarding in the ED while they wait for available inpatient beds. If a patient is waiting for an inpatient bed—whether from the ED, a postoperative recovery room, or a referring doctor's office—it implies that there are not enough inpatient beds to meet demand. In this scenario, the inpatient bed is the bottleneck. Typically, a stroll through the hospital would reveal inpatient rooms with clean, staffed, empty beds waiting to be filled—despite these beds being the bottleneck. The bottleneck is sitting idle. Exploiting the bottleneck means reducing or eliminating the time that an inpatient bed is empty.

Additionally, if a patient occupies an inpatient bed beyond the amount of time that is medically necessary, then the bottleneck is not being effectively exploited. For example, patients often remain in their beds long after they have been discharged while waiting for a ride home, waiting for prescriptions, or waiting on the nurse to review instructions. The patient could also be ready for discharge but waiting on an order from the treating physician. If a patient is ready for discharge in the morning but the physician doesn't write the discharge order until the afternoon, then the bottleneck has been functionally idle for hours. The most significant delays, however, come from patients who are medically ready for discharge but are waiting for an available community bed in a skilled nursing facility, assisted living facility, or adult foster home. Patients often wait weeks or months (and occasionally years) for an appropriate community bed to open up, remaining in the hospital long after their acute care needs have been met.

Let's examine a process map of patient flow that focuses on the inpatient side. Exhibit 3.4 highlights our need to create more granular process maps outlining the

Exhibit 3.4: Process Map of Patient Flow in the Inpatient Unit

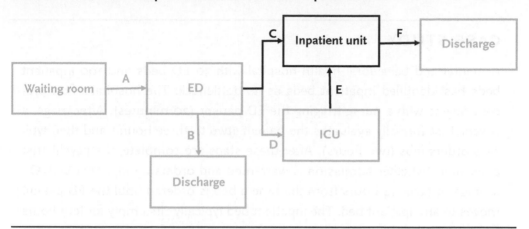

steps specifically where the bottleneck resource is used (Inpatient Unit) as well as immediately upstream (arrows C, E) and downstream (F) of the bottleneck. Most hospitals have a significant number of inpatient admissions from sources other than the ED (e.g., elective surgeries, outside hospital transfers, direct admissions), so it might also make sense to include an upstream step that represents an inflow of patients from these other sources (if these other sources represent a significant volume in your hospital).

When the inpatient bed is the bottleneck, coordinating admissions with the operating room schedule is important, but we recommend considering it as an entirely separate project. The busiest day of an elective surgery schedule is often the busiest day in the ED as well. Competition for a scarce inpatient bed can be one of the biggest contributors to idle time on the bottleneck, because inpatient beds are routinely held open for patients coming from surgery. Conversely, elective surgeries are often the biggest source of revenue for a hospital, and cancelling or delaying elective cases due to a lack of inpatient beds can have devastating financial consequences. TOC can effectively coordinate these competing demands, but tackling surgical flow has its own unique challenges. Therefore, it is probably best to hold off on making changes to the OR workflow until you have more expertise in implementing TOC.

To summarize, in the second focusing step we have made the decision to exploit the bottleneck by declaring that there will be no downtime on the bottleneck. This decision creates a mandate for change and codifies the adjustments that the hospital system will need to make to exploit the bottleneck. The second and third steps of the 5FS work closely together. The next focusing step discusses how to reorganize (subordinate) workflow to exploit the bottleneck.

Let's look at a case study.

CASE STUDY

A mental and behavioral health hospital with 30 ED beds and 100 inpatient beds has identified inpatient beds as its bottleneck. The hospital's flow process begins with a nurse triaging the ED patient (20 minutes). After triage, a psychiatrist formally evaluates the patient (two to three hours) and then typically orders labs (two hours). After these steps are complete, the psychiatrist determines whether admission is warranted and orders an inpatient bed. On average, it takes 14 hours from the time a bed is ordered until the ED patient moves to an inpatient bed. The inpatient bed typically sits empty for four hours before the patient arrives. The intake process (triage, formal evaluation, labs) can take five or six hours, but most patients who need to be admitted are identified as such during the initial triage process or early in the psychiatric evaluation. The decision to admit a patient is rarely swayed by completing the formal evaluation and lab testing.

How much downtime does the bottleneck resource have, and how can we exploit the bottleneck?

Intuitively, it may seem like the patient flow processes that occur in the ED—namely intake, evaluation, and disposition—could run more efficiently. However, in the case study, the bottleneck (an inpatient bed) lies *outside* of the ED, so improving the processes that take place *within* the ED may not be effective. Remember that an hour saved on a nonbottleneck is a mirage: Saving time on a nonbottleneck does not affect productivity, and in some cases, it will create more works-in-process that hinder flow.

It takes an average of 14 hours to move an admitted patient out of the ED after the bed order has been placed, and for much of that time, the bed the admitted patient will eventually move into is unavailable. The bed does, however, sit empty for an average of four hours. If the bed is clean and staffed during those four hours, then there are four hours of downtime on the bottleneck. Exploiting the bottleneck requires filling the bed with another admitted patient as soon as the bed is clean and staffed. We will return to this case study and discuss *how* to exploit the bottleneck in the next chapter.

SUMMARY

- Exploiting the bottleneck means eliminating (or minimizing) any idle time on the bottleneck.
- Any time lost on the bottleneck is time lost for the entire system.
- Create detailed process maps of the steps immediately upstream of the bottleneck, within the bottleneck, and immediately downstream of the bottleneck.
- Use these detailed maps to identify when and why the bottleneck sits idle.
- Create policy that mandates workflow changes to support exploitation of the bottleneck.

CHAPTER 4

The Third Focusing Step: Subordinate Everything to the Bottleneck

---

OBJECTIVES

- Reorganize workflow to subordinate everything else to the bottleneck
- Understand the impact of statistical fluctuations and dependent events on flow
- Recognize the importance of breaking down silos

IN THE SECOND FOCUSING STEP, we identified opportunities to exploit the bottleneck; we must now reorganize the system to capture these opportunities. The third focusing step is often the most difficult of the 5FS because it challenges the status quo and forces us to change the way we do things. Most hospital departments are not accustomed to operating for the greater good of the entire system. Departments are often siloed, and leaders may only be held accountable for their own turf. Local optima are rewarded, and department heads lack incentives to make sacrifices that benefit the system as a whole.

I (Chris) once worked with a hospital system that underwent cost-cutting measures to address a shortfall in its operating margin. Several departments made cuts in staffing—most notably social work, utilization management, and housekeeping—which eliminated positions and reduced their overall full-time equivalent hours. I have no doubt that the leaders of these departments were following orders to cut their budgets. Department heads are penalized or rewarded, to some extent, based on their ability to sufficiently reduce costs. While budget cuts will reduce expenses within the siloed departments, however, they may result in lost revenue for the hospital overall. Net revenue for the entire hospital is, of course, hospital leadership's true concern. Individual departmental balance sheets do not drive the financial health of a hospital system.

Suppose we wanted to determine if the departmental budget cuts are a productive move for the hospital: Will cutting staff fix the hospital's operating shortfall? To make such a determination, let's see how the staff cuts affect our three operational measurements: throughput, inventory, and operating expense.

- *Throughput.* If the social work, utilization management, and housekeeping departments were overstaffed (e.g., employees spent long stretches of time sitting idle, positions were redundant), then reducing staff should have no appreciable effect on throughput. However, as you can imagine, the departments were not overstaffed. Employees in these departments were usually busy. Moreover, housekeeping in particular had significant turnover and was occasionally short-staffed even before the cuts. We would therefore expect staffing cuts to decrease throughput.
- *Inventory.* With fewer housekeeping staff members, room turnover will likely take longer. As a result, patients who are waiting for beds will be boarding in other areas of the hospital, such as postoperative recovery rooms and the ED, and wait times will get longer, leading to an increase in inventory. Likewise, with fewer social workers, it will be more difficult to evaluate mental and behavioral health patients in a timely manner, especially in the ED. These patients in particular require complex discharge planning (e.g., scheduling follow-up appointments, finding substance abuse treatment programs, confirming community case management involvement, arranging temporary housing), which can be time-consuming. Without adequate social work and utilization management resources, these patients will board in the ED for long, unnecessary hours—leading to further increases in inventory.
- *Operating expense.* Reducing staff head count will initially reduce operating expense, but over time, decreased throughput and increased inventory will lead to increased costs. Staffing cuts will also make housekeeping and social work jobs more challenging, as employees who remain in their positions will have to do the same amount of work with less help. Higher staff turnover is a likely result, and it may drive further increases in operating expense, given the added costs of recruiting, hiring, and training new personnel.

Staff reductions are clearly a nonproductive move for the hospital: They will decrease throughput, increase inventory, and probably increase operating expense. Think of the situation this way: At some point, the resultant increase in ED boarding will necessitate ambulance diversion. The case study in chapter 2 estimated that one hour of ambulance diversion costs a hospital $10,000 in revenue.

If staffing cuts cause the ED to go on diversion as few as eight hours in one year, then any payroll savings from a full-time equivalent reduction could be erased. Staff reductions could also repeatedly delay operating room start times; surgeries could get postponed, and eventually surgeons and their patients would choose other hospitals for elective cases. The financial impact on the hospital could be significant.

Here's the challenge: The directors of social work, utilization management, and housekeeping are accountable for the cost of staff in their own departments, but they aren't accountable for the potential loss in hospital revenue that results from staffing cuts—nor should they be. It is easy to measure how much a department spends on employees but harder to measure the number of patients who aren't admitted or revenue that isn't collected. In a system of siloed departments, it is not easy to hold people accountable.

The hospital system needs to collectively adopt a new way of thinking; such a shift requires asking the staff to change, which can be difficult. In order to change, people need to understand why change is necessary, what needs to change, what their new reality will look like, and the risks of both making and not making changes.

Helping people understand the importance of change requires leadership to put forth tremendous effort. All staff must be appropriately educated—directors, managers, and frontline employees. Creating cultural change is the most complicated part of any flow endeavor; ignoring or minimizing its importance usually results in failure.

The second focusing step required a commitment to exploiting the bottleneck resource. In the third focusing step, we must determine how to achieve that exploitation. In a hospital setting, this requires making changes to the hospital's workflow that reduce idle time on the bottleneck while subordinating everything else in the system, including silos, standard operating procedures, local optimization, and short-term gains.

Back to the Drinking Fountain

In chapter 3, we used the example of a busy drinking fountain during recess to illustrate a system with a bottleneck. Certain "standard operating procedures" of the water fountain contribute to the bottleneck (e.g., the fountain is first-come, first-served; kids can spend as much time as they want at the fountain even if they aren't drinking from it). In the second focusing step, we decided to minimize idle time at the drinking fountain. Now, in the third focusing step, we must subordinate everything, including the way kids have used water fountains since the dawn of time, to exploiting the bottleneck.

To exploit the bottleneck, we need to explore ways that we can change the workflow at the drinking fountain (subordinate) to minimize downtime on the fountain:

- Make the kids start their water breaks earlier in the recess.
- Give kids reservations for the drinking fountain.
- Give the yard teacher a stopwatch to limit each child's time at the fountain.
- Develop an alarm system to limit each child's time at the fountain.
- Have an inventory of cups available so the kids can drink water away from the fountain.

Some of these possibilities may seem ridiculous for a playground, but if you substitute a hospital bed for the drinking fountain, the ideas may sound more familiar to you. Starting water breaks earlier in recess is comparable to discharging patients before noon. Reservations at the fountain are analogous to scheduling elective procedures and surgeries. The yard teacher with a stopwatch. . . maybe that's just a playground thing (although Lean researchers have certainly conducted time studies in hospitals).

Before implementing one or more of the ideas to minimize downtime on the fountain, we need to evaluate the effectiveness of each idea. By anticipating the effect of each idea on throughput, inventory, and operating expense, we increase the likelihood of choosing solutions that will produce our desired results.

- *Make kids start their water breaks earlier in recess.* Assuming that kids who drink earlier won't want another drink at the end of recess, this idea could work. Earlier water breaks would reduce downtime on the bottleneck that occurs in the first part of recess, when most kids are too busy playing to get a drink of water (downtime on the bottleneck happens anytime the fountain sits idle, not just during a period of peak usage). Shifting use from later to earlier would therefore exploit the bottleneck. Throughput would improve as measured across the entire recess period; inventory would decrease because fewer kids would be standing in line at the end of recess, and operating expense would remain the same.
- *Give kids reservations for the drinking fountain.* Reserved drinking times yield the same results as the first scenario of having kids take drinks earlier in recess: Throughput increases, inventory decreases, and operating expense stays the same. Neither solution, however, ensures that kids are actually drinking from the fountain rather than just standing at it.
- *Limit the amount of time each child has at the fountain.* This is arguably one of the best subordinations to exploit the bottleneck. We need a system that

not only ensures no wasted time at the fountain but also has built-in aids to facilitate and maintain the changes we wish to implement. Examples of built-in aids include a yard teacher with a stopwatch, a drinking fountain alarm, and a supply of drinking cups. All three system changes subordinate everything else to the bottleneck, reduce idle time on the bottleneck, and improve throughput.

When you change the way processes typically play out, you subordinate the status quo in order to improve flow through the bottleneck—in other words, you change procedures and common practices to support exploitation.

Revisiting the Mattel Factory

We can also subordinate processes to the bottleneck in the Mattel factory. The bottleneck in Barbie production is at the right-arm station. In chapter 3, we identified potential idle time on the bottleneck, and exhibit 3.1 offers insight into how to exploit the bottleneck. By looking at the locations just upstream of the bottleneck (A), just downstream of the bottleneck (B), and at the bottleneck itself (right-arm station), we can identify ways to change the current operating procedures and reduce downtime on the bottleneck. Upstream, we need to protect the bottleneck from running out of material to work on so that it can continue to assemble the right arms. We must ensure that temporary production glitches don't result in too few left-armed Barbies reaching the right-arm station, thereby starving the bottleneck. We can mitigate the risk by maintaining a small surplus of inventory, known as a buffer, in front of the bottleneck. We can also start producing parts for left-armed Barbies earlier in the process so that they arrive at the bottleneck sooner. Earlier production allows for the identification and correction of potential delays before they become a problem. In the event of a slowdown in left-armed Barbie production, the bottleneck will still have adequate inventory from the buffer to continue production.

Other potential problems and solutions include the following:

- *Idle time on the bottleneck as a result of staff breaks.* If everyone at the right-arm station takes a break at the same time, the bottleneck will fall idle. The solution is to stagger breaks so there is always someone to work at the bottleneck.
- *Idle time on the bottleneck as a result of routine maintenance.* The solution is to schedule maintenance on the bottleneck station during nights and weekends, when the plant isn't operating.

As a general rule, you never want to take the bottleneck station offline when it could be running. Of course, before implementing any solution, you must test it to see whether the action will increase throughput, reduce inventory, and reduce operating expense.

SUBORDINATING TO THE BOTTLENECK IN HOSPITAL SYSTEMS

Let's revisit the process map in exhibit 2.1 to see how to apply the third focusing step to a hospital system. Once you've identified the bottleneck in exhibit 2.1, you will want to create a more granular process map that details the bottleneck resource and its immediate upstream and downstream processes (see exhibits 2.2, 3.1, and 3.3 for examples).

The granular process maps should make clear when the bottleneck is sitting idle—and why. Keep your focus on processes that immediately feed into or supply the bottleneck (i.e., immediate upstream processes), the bottleneck resource itself, and processes that are fed directly by the bottleneck (i.e., immediate downstream processes). Subordinating everything to the bottleneck requires you to examine and change operations in these three areas. To do so, you must eliminate, shorten, or rearrange the current processes. Elimination is often the easiest change to implement, because it involves a simple work reduction. Rearranging steps is often the most difficult method of change.

Let's return to our example of a hospital system in which the inpatient bed is the bottleneck resource. We will create a granular process map to identify opportunities to eliminate, shorten, or rearrange steps upstream of the bottleneck, at the bottleneck, and downstream of the bottleneck. Upstream, the bottleneck is most likely to be idle when an inpatient bed is clean but sits empty, waiting for a new patient from another department—the ED, the ICU, or an outside hospital, for example. Downstream, the bottleneck is most likely to sit idle when a patient who is medically ready for discharge still occupies an inpatient bed—either because there is a delay in writing a discharge order or because the discharge order has been written but not carried out. Exhibit 4.1 depicts the bottleneck and its upstream and downstream processes. Arrows C, E, and E' are the immediate upstream steps of the bottleneck, representing admissions from the ED, ICU, and OR (or transfers in), respectively; F is the immediate downstream step, representing discharge from the unit.

In our example, there is significant idle time at the bottleneck when an inpatient bed sits empty. Meanwhile, the upstream units have an excessive number of boarded patients waiting to be transferred to inpatient beds. Therefore, one focus for procedural change should be at C of exhibit 4.1, where ED patients are

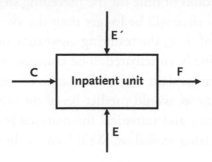

admitted to the inpatient unit. We now need to create a more granular process map of C (exhibit 4.2).

The process begins with the decision to admit an ED patient. The physician orders a bed, which triggers a request at bed control. The request is then sent to the house supervisor, who looks for an appropriate inpatient bed. The supervisor discusses the admission with the charge nurse of the appropriate inpatient unit, and the charge nurse reviews the patient's ED chart. After further discussion, the charge nurse approves or denies the bed, and the supervisor relays this decision to bed control. If the bed is approved, the patient is assigned to the bed. If the bed is not approved, the process begins again with a new inpatient unit. Meanwhile, the bed under consideration, which is the bottleneck resource, sits empty. Whew!

The process laid out in exhibit 4.2 allows us to quantify how much time each activity in the process takes. We can then streamline the process based on the amount of time we anticipate for each activity and the ease or difficulty of implementing proposed changes.

It is important to consider not only the average but also the maximum and minimum amount of time each step may take. Each step in the process is dependent on completion of the preceding step—bed control can't look for a bed until it receives a request; the house supervisor can't talk to the charge nurse until the

Exhibit 4.2: Workflow of Patient Admission from ED to Inpatient Unit

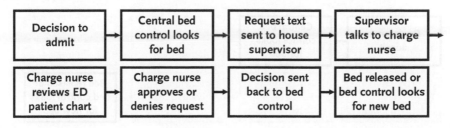

request is sent from bed control, and so on. Although a subsequent step will generally wait the average amount of time for the preceding step to be completed, there is a chance that the wait time will be longer than the average. If several steps take the maximum amount of time, the resulting downtime on the bottleneck may be much longer than originally anticipated. The concepts of dependent events and statistical fluctuations can explain why such a series of steps will accumulate slowness far in excess of what we would predict based on average wait times. Understanding dependent events and statistical fluctuations is crucial to making smart decisions about reorganizing workflow. We'll look at these concepts more closely in a minute.

Eliminating Activities

Intuitively, exhibit 4.2 seems to have more steps than necessary, with each step delaying the placement of a patient in an inpatient bed and adding idle time to the bottleneck. We can easily eliminate a few steps from the process. In most cases, the ED physician has a good sense of the type of bed or unit that the patient will need and can confirm this with the accepting physician. Bed control knows which beds are available, so we can cut out the middlemen—the house supervisor and the charge nurse—and streamline the process for acquiring an inpatient bed. In exhibit 4.3, we have reduced the number of activities from eight to three. The time saved from eliminating steps (subordination) translates to improved use of the bottleneck (exploitation).

Shortening Activities

So far, we have addressed only half of C in exhibit 4.1. Although we have streamlined the process of acquiring an inpatient bed, we still must consider the process by which a patient physically moves from the ED to the inpatient unit. Exhibit 4.4 describes this process.

Exhibit 4.3: Streamlined Workflow of Patient Admission from ED to Inpatient Unit

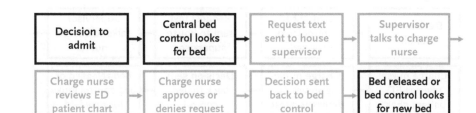

Exhibit 4.4: Workflow from Bed Assignment to Transfer of Care to Inpatient Unit

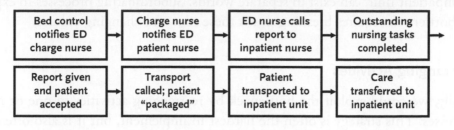

Once an ED patient has been assigned to an inpatient bed, bed control notifies the ED charge nurse, who notifies the ED staff nurse caring for that patient. The ED nurse gives report to the accepting inpatient nurse, completes any outstanding orders, and finishes charting; the ED nurse then calls for transport and packages up the patient. Transport arrives, takes the patient to the new bed, and care is transferred to the inpatient unit.

Because the current workflow for transfer of care includes eight discrete activities, the process can create significant downtime on the bottleneck. Unlike exhibit 4.2, none of the activities in exhibit 4.4 can be easily eliminated; however, several can be shortened. For example, the ED nurse is supposed to give report to the inpatient nurse, but there is no guarantee that the ED nurse will be ready when the bed is assigned. Likewise, the inpatient nurse may not be available to receive report. The inpatient floor could be busy with other admissions, or the inpatient nurse could be on a break. In the current workflow, neither the ED nor the accepting unit is obligated to transfer the patient within a specific time frame. One solution is to subordinate this activity to the bottleneck by mandating that report is given and received within 15 minutes of bed assignment.

If resources that are necessary to support the bottleneck are occupied with a nonbottleneck issue, then the bottleneck will sit idle. In our example of inpatient bed assignments, the inpatient nurse was not available to receive report on an admitted patient from the ED. This scenario illustrates a nonbottleneck (the inpatient nurse) not being available to support the bottleneck (an available inpatient bed). The nonbottleneck temporarily becomes a new bottleneck. There must be a system in place to prevent this possibility and to ensure that the activities needed to support the bottleneck are available.

Similarly, if transport is unavailable, we would need to alter workflow to circumvent the transport delay and minimize downtime on the bottleneck resource. One possibility is for an ED tech or nurse to transport the patient to the inpatient unit. Another is for an inpatient nurse to come to the ED and collect the patient.

You can see how shortening activities is more difficult than eliminating activities altogether. Asking people to do their jobs differently requires changing their expectations. When a hospital is siloed, different departments, such as the ED and the inpatient unit, can exist in separate worlds. Subordinating processes to exploit the bottleneck requires breaking down these silos and changing culture.

Rearranging Activities

Finally, we could exploit the bottleneck by rearranging activities in one or more processes. This strategy is often the hardest to implement, but it is also often the most effective. To understand why, we must first understand dependent events and statistical fluctuations. These phenomena often render workflow unacceptably slow; rearranging steps in that workflow can mitigate the slowness.[1]

DEPENDENT EVENTS AND STATISTICAL FLUCTUATIONS

Dependent events occur whenever a workflow has a series of linear events in which each step depends on the completion of the preceding step. Statistical fluctuations are variations in the time each individual step can take to complete from one instance to the next. When dependent events and statistical fluctuations exist in a system, flow can take an unacceptably long time.

Driving in traffic is a great illustration of dependent events and statistical fluctuations. Let's return to the example of chauffeuring my (Chris's) kids to and from school. Suppose I leave my house to pick up one of my children. On the way to the school, I pull onto the main road and merge into a line of cars. A stoplight turns red, and I'm 10 cars away from the light. There are 50 yards between me and the intersection, and the speed limit is 30 miles per hour. Theoretically, when the light turns green, it should take me about four seconds to get through the intersection. But we all know it won't play out that way.

I won't make the next light because of dependent events and statistical fluctuations. When the light turns green, I can't simply step on the gas and go; I have to wait for the car in front of me to move. The car in front of me must wait for the car in front of it, and so on. Imagine all 10 cars in the line as a series of activities in a workflow process. Each car's ability to move forward depends on the movement of the car in front of it. In other words, traffic moving through the green light is a series of dependent events. The starting point of each activity is the preceding activity's endpoint, plus lag time. The longer the series of activities, the longer the wait will be. If each car takes an average of 20 seconds to get through the light, and if there are nine cars in front of me and each car has to wait for the car in front of it, then I will wait, on average, 180 seconds until it is my turn. That's three minutes of wait time, and it means that I'm probably not making the light.

But wait! We also need to factor in statistical fluctuations. In our example, each car takes an average of 20 seconds to get through the light, but that doesn't mean each car will actually take 20 seconds. Some cars will take less time; some will take more. Most will take more. If the driver in the first car is texting, he won't notice when the light turns green. The driver in the second car starts honking her horn, which angers the first driver. By the time the first driver puts down the phone, screams out the window at the second driver, and goes through the light, close to a minute has passed. With road rage bubbling, the second driver screams back for an extra few seconds before going through the light. The third car stalls. Now several minutes have passed, and only two cars have made it through the intersection. The line of traffic is moving much more slowly than the average of 20 seconds per car. I should be halfway to the intersection but I'm not even close to moving.

Statistical fluctuations occur because although each discrete event takes an average amount of time in the aggregate, when considered individually, the amount of time can vary quite a bit. The amount of time an event (e.g., a car making it through the light) takes may be faster than the average or slower than the average. Unfortunately, the net effect is that events move more slowly overall—usually much more slowly.

The reason is that although one event may take less time than the average, the time savings may not be passed on to subsequent events. In a series of dependent events, even if a preceding activity is completed more quickly than expected, the next activity may not be ready to begin. In exhibit 4.4—the process of moving a patient from the ED to an inpatient unit—bed control takes an average of 20 minutes to assign a bed and notify the ED charge nurse. A bed could be assigned in as little as five minutes, which seems to save time. However, if bed control can't reach the ED charge nurse, it doesn't matter how quickly the bed is assigned. The activities in exhibit 4.4 are dependent events, and the activities that follow charge nurse notification cannot begin until the charge nurse has been notified.

This example illustrates an additional point about the slowness that dependent events and statistical fluctuations introduce into a system. The nature of tasks is that the time to complete them normally has a long tail. Time is bounded on the left side; there is a finite amount of time that can be saved by competing the task early. It is *not* bounded on the right side, however; the task can be delayed by an infinite amount of time. The net result is that relatively long delays usually occur. We see this in my drive to the school: The fastest I can go through the light if I tailgate the car in front of me might be five seconds, which shaves only seconds off the average. The potential time savings is bounded. The longest it will take me depends on when the third car's tow truck shows up. That could take all day; it is not bounded.

To summarize: In a series of dependent events, each event must wait for the preceding event to finish before it can begin. Each event's starting point is the preceding event's endpoint plus lag time, so the longer the series of events is, the longer the wait will be. The potential for each event to take longer than the average is much greater than the potential for taking less time, and the net result is an accumulation of slowness. Each event must wait for the delays of all preceding steps *combined* before it can begin! Sitting 10 cars back, I'm going to be delayed by the amount of time the first car was delayed, plus the amount of time the second car was delayed, plus the amount of time the third car was delayed, and so on. I'll never get to the school on time!

Returning to exhibit 4.4, if the ED charge nurse is available as soon as bed control calls, the bed can be assigned in as little as five minutes, and the system has saved 15 minutes. However, this activity takes only 20 minutes on average, so the maximum amount of time that can be saved is relatively small. On the other hand, there is virtually an infinite amount of delay that can occur in the system. The best-case scenario may be that it takes 5 minutes instead of 20 minutes to assign the bed and notify the charge nurse. In the worst-case scenario, the hospital is full and it takes days to find the patient a bed. Even though 20 minutes is the average time spent on this activity, the potential for delay is vastly greater than the potential for catching up from delays—the potential delay is not bounded—and the same dynamic exists for every activity in the process.

A hospital is an incredibly complex system with many dependent events and statistical fluctuations. Coupled with the sheer volume of patients, relatively small delays on individual dependent steps can translate into a tremendous amount of downtime on a bottleneck. Conversely, making a few workflow changes that better control dependencies and fluctuations can free up considerable capacity on the bottleneck. Now that we understand this paradigm, we can rearrange steps in a workflow to mitigate the accumulation of slowness.

Dependent Events and Statistical Fluctuation in the ED

Let's examine how dependent events and statistical fluctuation affect patient flow when the bottleneck is an ED bed.

Exhibit 4.5 depicts patient flow through the ED, beginning when the patient checks in and ending when the patient leaves the ED. The average time for each step in the workflow is listed on the diagram. The average ED length of stay (using the average totals of all steps combined) is 248 minutes. The minimum length of stay is 49 minutes, which might be typical of a low-acuity patient who needs minimal testing, is easily discharged, and arrives at the ED during a nonpeak period (e.g., a patient who comes in with an ankle sprain in the early afternoon). The maximum length of stay is 838 minutes. In a series of dependent events with statistical fluctuations, the opportunity for slowness or delay is much greater than

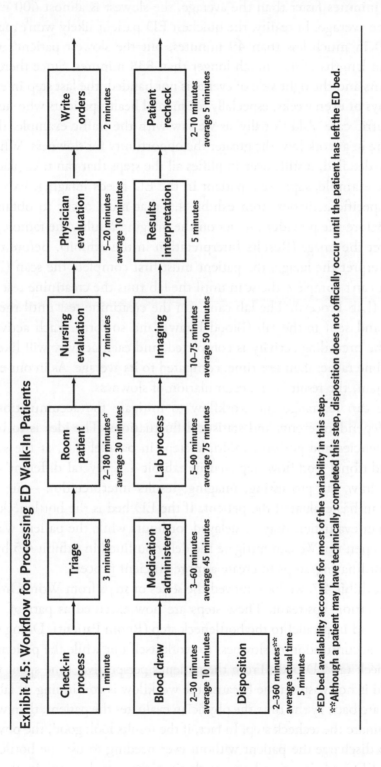

Exhibit 4.5: Workflow for Processing ED Walk-In Patients

Check-in process — 1 minute

Triage — 3 minutes

Room patient — 2–180 minutes* average 30 minutes

Nursing evaluation — 7 minutes

Physician evaluation — 5–20 minutes average 10 minutes

Write orders — 2 minutes

Blood draw — 2–30 minutes average 10 minutes

Medication administered — 3–60 minutes average 45 minutes

Lab process — 5–90 minutes average 75 minutes

Imaging — 10–75 minutes average 50 minutes

Results interpretation — 5 minutes

Patient recheck — 2–10 minutes average 5 minutes

Disposition — 2–360 minutes** average actual time 5 minutes

*ED bed availability accounts for most of the variability in this step.

**Although a patient may have technically completed this step, disposition does not officially occur until the patient has left the ED bed.

the opportunity to make up for lost time. While the quickest ED patient workflow is 200 minutes faster than the average, the slowest is almost 600 minutes longer than the average. In reality, the quickest ED patient likely won't make it through the ED in much less than 49 minutes, but the slowest patient's workflow will result in lengths of stay much longer than 838 minutes. Since there is a long tail on events and the right side of events is not banded, the last step in exhibit 4.5 can take days or even weeks, especially for mental health patients who need specialized psychiatric care. Additionally, as we saw with the traffic example, the more steps there are in a workflow, the greater the opportunity for slowness. While exhibit 4.5 is fairly detailed, it still oversimplifies all the steps that can take place in ED care.

For example, suppose a patient in the ED needs imaging. Exhibit 4.6 shows those specific activities from exhibit 4.5 that must occur to obtain an imaging scan. Before the provider can act on the imaging results, the radiologist must first interpret the image (Results Interpretation in the exhibit). Before the radiologist can interpret the image, the patient must first complete the scan (Imaging). The patient can't complete the scan until the lab runs the creatinine test and posts the results (Lab Process). The lab can't run the creatinine test until the blood is collected and sent to the lab (Blood Draw), and so forth. Each activity must wait until the preceding activity is completed, and each activity will likely take much more time rather than less time, compared to its average. As in our example of the traffic jam, the result is an accumulation of slowness.

We can rearrange the workflow to mitigate the accumulation of slowness from dependent events and statistical fluctuations. The idea is to break assumed dependencies and perform multiple steps in parallel (i.e., at the same time). In the traditional workflow depicted in exhibit 4.5, several different steps—orders, blood draw, lab processing, imaging, results interpretation—must wait until a physician has evaluated the patient. If the ED bed is the bottleneck resource, the physician evaluation may be delayed for hours while the patient waits for an ED bed to open up. We can mitigate the delay outlined in exhibit 4.5 by rearranging, or subordinating, steps to create a more efficient process.

In exhibit 4.7, we have moved the series of steps from Write Orders to Results Interpretation upstream. These steps are now executed as part of, or soon after, Triage, and in parallel to the bottleneck step (Room Patient). Doing so allows time for any accumulation of slowness to work itself out while the patient waits for the bottleneck (an ED bed). From the patient's perspective, time spent waiting for an ED bed is not wasted time because the workflow is continuing. If lab and imaging results are back by the time the physician evaluates the patient, then we may be able to eliminate the recheck step. In fact, if the results look good, the physician may be able to discharge the patient without ever needing to use the bottleneck resource of the ED bed. Imagine how much time that would save! In the conventional

Exhibit 4.6: Workflow for Obtaining an Imaging Scan in the ED

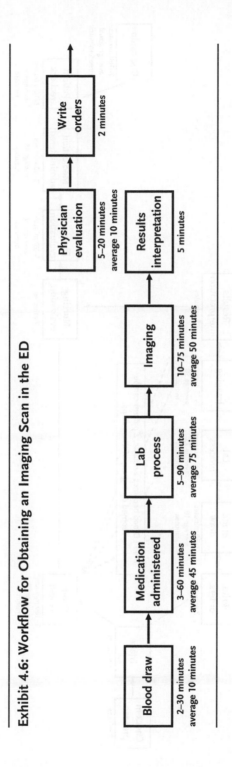

Exhibit 4.7: Revised ED Workflow with Steps Moved Upstream of the Bottleneck

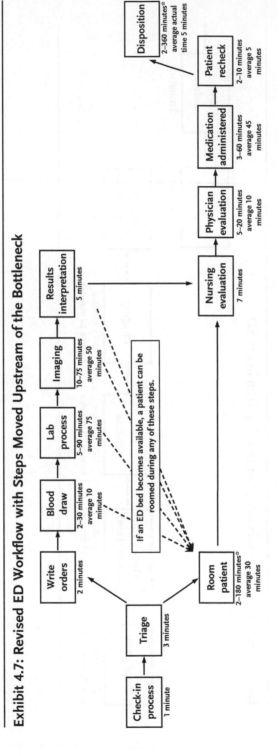

*Although a patient may have technically completed this step, disposition does not officially occur until the patient has left the ED bed.

workflow of exhibit 4.5, if it takes 180 minutes to room a patient, and all other steps take the average amount of time, the patient's ED length of stay is 398 minutes. By rearranging the steps as outlined in exhibit 4.7, the patient has labs drawn and imaging studies completed before being roomed. In the revised workflow, the start time for rooming a patient begins after triage and occurs *in parallel* with other activities, specifically Write Orders, Blood Draw, Lab Process, Imaging, and Results Interpretation (and by the way, the patient can be moved out of the waiting room anytime an ED bed becomes available). We have broken the dependency on rooming the patient, and the parallel activities that take an average of 142 minutes are being completed *during* the 180 minutes that the patient is waiting to be roomed rather than after. Now, instead of a 398-minute ED length of stay (4 minutes for Check In and Triage, 180 minutes to Room Patient, and 214 minutes on average for the remaining steps), the patient's length of stay has been reduced to 256 minutes (4 minutes for Check In and Triage, 180 minutes to Room Patient, during which time the parallel activities are being completed, and 72 minutes on average for the remaining steps). Rearranging steps and breaking the dependency on the bottleneck saves 142 minutes per patient on a busy day when waits for an available ED room are long. Since an ED treats a high volume of patients each day, this single process change can free up a tremendous amount of capacity on the bottleneck!

MORE EXAMPLES OF SUBORDINATION

Subordination Downstream of the Bottleneck

Up to now, our examples of eliminating, shortening, and rearranging workflow steps have focused on events upstream of the bottleneck, but we can subordinate events downstream of the bottleneck as well. Returning to the inpatient bed as the bottleneck in exhibit 4.1, the events downstream of the bottleneck are represented at F. Delays in those events may contribute to downtime on the bottleneck—for example, if a patient is medically ready for discharge but does not have a discharge order; if a patient has a discharge order but has not been officially discharged; if a patient has been discharged but has not physically left the room; or if a patient room is empty but not yet assigned to a new patient.

Each downstream event can be subdivided into more granular activities that must be reviewed and potentially eliminated, shortened, or rearranged. Downstream workflow could be rearranged by having physicians round first on the patients who may be discharged that day; writing orders for discharge medications early in the morning; ordering final laboratory tests the night before so that results will be available on the morning of a patient's anticipated discharge; providing frequent updates to patients and families to help them arrange and coordinate transport upon discharge; and setting expectations for how long it should take nurses to discharge patients after receiving discharge orders. These are just examples and not meant to be turnkey solutions. Applying the focusing steps to your hospital's specific circumstances will illuminate your specific opportunities for reducing wait times.

Other examples for subordination downstream of the bottleneck include the following:

- Work with ED charge nurses to ensure that no clean, staffed beds are held open for unexpected codes or traumas. If all ED beds are full and a new, critical patient arrives at the ED, other patients can almost always be moved to make a room available for the critical patient.
- Streamline the process for requesting and assigning inpatient beds. Do not hold inpatient beds empty for future needs, such as elective surgeries that won't finish for hours or transfers from other hospitals that won't arrive till the next day. Improve the communication between ED and inpatient nurses and physicians to coordinate inpatient bed assignments.
- Develop a system to effectively identify which beds should be cleaned first. Housekeeping staff should be flexible and able to travel between units and floors based on which beds need to be cleaned next.
- Explore setting up a discharge lounge, especially if patients who have been discharged but are still occupying inpatient beds are creating significant downtime on the bottleneck.
- Allow an ED physician to write holding orders or transition orders for admitted patients rather than waiting for an admitting physician to come to the ED, evaluate the patient, and write orders.
- Make sure that ED physicians and accepting physicians (in consultation with nurses) understand the level of care and type of bed that a patient needs at the time of bed request. Coordination on these issues avoids delays in bed assignment.

Remember that any move should address your particular bottleneck by reducing or eliminating waste that is currently preventing you from exploiting the bottleneck.

At this point in the process, many hospital flow teams become prematurely concerned with collecting data—what kinds of data they need to collect, how detailed the data should be, and whether complete data sets are needed before getting started. Although data can help you decide what changes to make and track the effectiveness of those changes, don't let incomplete data prevent you from beginning the 5FS. Your data do not need to be particularly sophisticated or complicated, especially early in your flow endeavors. Data should point to the biggest opportunities for improvement and, once you determine which variables you need to track, indicate the degree to which your efforts are successful.

Let's return to the case study from chapter 3.

CASE STUDY

A mental and behavioral health hospital with 30 ED beds and 100 inpatient beds has identified inpatient beds as its bottleneck. The hospital's flow process begins with a nurse triaging the ED patient (20 minutes). After triage, a psychiatrist formally evaluates the patient (two to three hours) and then typically orders lab tests (two hours). After these steps are complete, the psychiatrist determines whether admission is warranted and orders an inpatient bed. On average, it takes 14 hours from the time a bed is ordered until the ED patient moves to an inpatient bed. The inpatient bed typically sits empty for four hours before the patient arrives. The intake process (triage, formal evaluation, labs) can take five or six hours, but most patients who need to be admitted are identified as such during the initial triage process or early in the psychiatric evaluation. The decision to admit a patient is rarely swayed by completing the formal evaluation and lab testing.

How much downtime does the bottleneck resource have, and how can we exploit the bottleneck?

In chapter 3, we determined that we could eliminate idle time on the bottleneck by moving an ED patient into an inpatient bed as soon as one becomes available. To do so, we streamlined the process whereby the inpatient physician reviews and accepts the ED patient for admission and reduced delays in nursing reports.

We could also reorganize the workflow upstream of the bottleneck. It would be most effective to move the activities that take the longest amount of time—the bed request and bed assignment—earlier in the process. Since it is usually apparent during triage if a patient will ultimately need admission, we can make a bed request part of the triage process. By doing so, subsequent activities, along with their associated accumulation of slowness, can occur while a patient bed is being requested and assigned—saving up to five and a half hours. If, after formal evaluation, the ED psychiatrist determines that the patient does not need admission, there is still time to cancel the bed request. While it may seem less efficient to begin a process that could ultimately prove unnecessary, the bed request is a nonbottleneck that can be subordinated to the bottleneck resource (an inpatient bed). Time saved on a nonbottleneck is a mirage.

As an aside, the mental health facility in the case study had a practice of not discharging patients during the weekend. By changing its practices to accommodate weekend discharges, the facility was able to free up additional capacity on the bottleneck.

Now here's a bonus case study highlighting subordination.

CASE STUDY

A 35-bed ED is built to manage 50,000 annual visits. Within two years, the ED's average annual volume has unexpectedly increased to 72,000 visits. The ED now needs 13 additional beds, but there is no capital for expansion. The admission rate of ED patients is only 15 percent and the hospital's inpatient units have sufficient capacity—the bottleneck resource is the ED bed. The average length of time a patient waits for an available ED bed is increasing, and the number of patients who leave the ED without being seen has become unacceptably high.

Through a joint effort, the ED physicians and nurses formalize a process to see all walk-in patients in the triage area before assignment to an ED bed. Physicians will quickly evaluate a patient, order appropriate tests and treatments, and then either have the patient wait for results in the waiting room or assign the patient to an ED bed (if the patient's acuity warrants use of the bottleneck resource). As soon as test results are available, physician assistants will reevaluate patients and either discharge them or send them to an ED bed. If the providers stick to the plan, the system works brilliantly. If an ED physician evaluates patients too slowly or does not hand off responsibility to a physician assistant—perhaps motivated to retain all the revenue from patient encounters—the system's performance suffers.

How does the new plan subordinate activities to the bottleneck?

Using exhibits 4.5 and 4.7 as templates, map out the basic ED workflow before and after the subordination. The plan outlined in the case study is called a provider-in-triage (PIT) model. It is a variation of split flow, in which patients are assigned either "vertical" status (they do not get assigned an ED bed) or "horizontal" status (they get placed in an ED bed as soon as possible) based on their presenting acuity. An ED "fast track" also illustrates the split-flow model. The underlying premise of a fast track is that there is a subset of products, known as "free products" in TOC vocabulary, that should never need the bottleneck resource. In the traditional workflow, the free products sit in a queue behind products that need the bottleneck; throughput is delayed when the subset must wait behind a resource it will never need. We can move free products out of the queue by creating a parallel workflow that does not involve the bottleneck. If an ED bed is the bottleneck, we can save time by treating and discharging lower-acuity patients who don't need an ED bed in a fast-track area of the ED. The fast-track workflow exists in parallel with the main ED workflow that treats sicker patients who need beds. In a traditional split-flow model, nurses usually triage patients to a fast-track (as opposed to higher-acuity) area. The PIT model works similarly, except that in a PIT, the ED physicians perform triage alongside nurses, not only deciding whom to fast-track but also writing orders, including discharge orders, directly from triage.

For a PIT model to work well, it needs uniform provider practices. If provider practices vary too much (e.g., providers move too slowly, are not comfortable making decisions after spending only a brief amount of time with patients, or hoard patients), then significant challenges may arise. In particular, providers who hoard patients defeat the purpose of the PIT model. Hoarding patients is equivalent to having too many works-in-process, which causes the physician to become a new bottleneck. Potential gains in throughput and inventory are never realized. To avoid detrimental practice variability, PIT practices must be standardized.

SUMMARY

- Subordination means changing the way things are currently done to minimize lost time on the bottleneck.
- Subordination can involve eliminating, shortening, and rearranging workflow steps immediately upstream of a bottleneck, at the bottleneck, and immediately downstream of the bottleneck.
- Subordination requires a culture change and a commitment to improving the system as a whole. Such a commitment involves breaking down silos and eliminating local optima.
- Rearranging workflow steps can mitigate the accumulation of slowness created by dependent events and statistical fluctuations.

NOTE

1. While eliminating and shortening steps are useful subordinating tools, rearranging steps in workflow is especially effective in overcoming the slowness that accumulates specifically from dependent events and statistical fluctuations.

CHAPTER 5

The Fourth Focusing Step:
Elevate the Bottleneck

OBJECTIVES

- Understand how to elevate the bottleneck
- Increase capacity of the bottleneck resource
- Reduce demand for the bottleneck resource

BY THIS POINT, you have learned how to exploit the bottleneck and, more important, how to subordinate everything else to the bottleneck and effectively change the status quo. Downtime on the bottleneck is now at a minimum, and the bottleneck is not only functioning around the clock but also working on the appropriate products. Despite these improvements to the system, however, there may still be insufficient capacity at the bottleneck resource. When a system consistently operates at more than 80–85 percent of capacity, it starts to lose efficiency, and its ability to absorb unexpected surges declines exponentially. Therefore, we should strive to reconfigure the bottleneck so that it maintains, on average, an excess capacity of 15 percent. The first three focusing steps may not be enough to smash the bottleneck. It's time to introduce the fourth focusing step: Elevate the bottleneck!

Elevating the bottleneck essentially means either adding capacity to the bottleneck or reducing demand for it. Reducing demand does not require turning patients away or avoiding new business opportunities; likewise, adding capacity does not necessarily require building a new hospital wing. Elevating the bottleneck does require some investment—usually of capital—so it is important to make sure the first three focusing steps have been optimized.

To see the fourth focusing step in action, let's revisit the drinking fountain on the playground. Prior to applying TOC, kids would run to the fountain when recess was almost over and form a first-come, first-served line. There was no time limit for how long a kid could spend at the fountain. This invariably meant that some kids couldn't get a drink before recess ended. In chapters 1–4, we used TOC to identify the reasons for downtime on the bottleneck and discussed ways of subordinating workflow to exploit the bottleneck. These actions have improved the situation at the drinking fountain, but it's likely that the workflow is still not optimal. We need to elevate the bottleneck.

To elevate the bottleneck, we could buy a second drinking fountain or replace the current fountain with a new one that has multiple faucets, allowing more than one child to drink at the same time. These solutions add capacity to the bottleneck. Alternatively, we could reduce demand for the fountain instead. A cheaper option could be to buy a rain catcher and some cups, and let the kids drink from "nature's fountain." We could also reduce demand by installing a cover over the playground: The shade will keep the kids cooler, so they will need less water. Our purpose in elevating the bottleneck is to eventually render it a nonbottleneck.

ELEVATING THE BOTTLENECK IN A HOSPITAL SETTING

In a hospital setting, many ways of elevating the bottleneck will not be practical or cost-effective. For example, if an inpatient hospital bed is the bottleneck, we could build more inpatient rooms, thereby increasing capacity, or transfer patients to another hospital in the health system instead of boarding them in the ED, thereby reducing demand. Neither solution is ideal; building new beds is a complicated and expensive process, and transferring patients to another hospital is essentially giving away business (imagine if McDonald's drove its customers to Burger King when the McDonald's lines got too long). Keeping practicality and cost-effectiveness in mind, we can examine how to elevate a constraint, or bottleneck, using previous examples of bottlenecks—inpatient beds and ED beds.

Add Capacity to Inpatient Beds

If an inpatient bed is the bottleneck, then adding more inpatient beds, or building more rooms, is perhaps the most obvious way to elevate the bottleneck. While such action may be appropriate in some instances, we can first undertake other, simpler measures to improve flow. Building beds is a costly and time-consuming strategy, and the strategy may be rendered irrelevant if it is undertaken in response to a transient surge in patient volume.

It is also possible that the third focusing step, in which we subordinate everything to the bottleneck, is not yet complete. In other words, we may not have done enough to increase throughput, and as a result, elevation of the bottleneck would be premature. If a hospital's inpatient units are still full of patients who aren't being discharged in a timely fashion, then adding more beds will not solve the problem. Rather than increasing throughput, adding capacity will instead increase inventory and operating expense. In chapter 1, we looked at a hospital that doubled its ED capacity, only to discover that increased capacity made flow worse.

Imagine a kitchen sink that has a clog in the drain—the water is about to overflow. Instead of completely removing the clog, we could instead buy a bigger sink. This would appear to improve the situation initially, but without removing the clog, the water will still overflow eventually (and the resulting mess will be even bigger). Buying a bigger sink—that is, elevating the bottleneck—is analogous to building more beds, and failing to remove the clog first means failing to exploit the bottleneck prior to investing in more capacity.

Additionally, before committing to a measure as disruptive and expensive as new construction, the nonbottleneck resources in your system must be prepared to accommodate increased capacity. Suppose new inpatient beds are built but sit empty because there aren't enough nurses to staff the beds or housekeepers to clean them. Increasing capacity may elevate the bottleneck, but it has also created a new bottleneck—staff members—who are significantly less expensive than new construction. When we contemplate adding capacity to a bottleneck, we must ensure that the nonbottleneck resources have enough excess capacity to support the new capacity on the bottleneck. If they do not, we must increase capacity on nonbottlenecks *prior to* increasing bottleneck capacity.

It sounds like adding more inpatient beds may not be the best solution right now. There are, however, other ways to increase the capacity of inpatient beds. For example, if there are enough patients who have short lengths of stay and need treatment that follows straightforward protocols (e.g., chest pain, cellulitis, asthma, and congestive heart failure exacerbations), we can convert part or all of an existing inpatient unit to an observation unit. If run properly, each bed in an observation unit can yield the same capacity as one-and-a-half to two inpatient beds.

Some hospitals add beds to the hallway of an inpatient unit and move admitted patients there instead of boarding them in the ED. Advocates of inpatient hallway beds point to literature showing that this practice increases patient satisfaction, decreases lengths of stay, and improves outcomes when strict inclusion criteria are followed. Hallway beds can be particularly effective at increasing the functional capacity of inpatient units during times of volume surge.

Hospitals may also use flex units, which are extra patient units that are closed when volumes are low and open during periods of sustained higher volumes. Flex units are especially helpful in elevating the bottleneck when patient volumes are predictably higher, such as flu season, because hospitals can also plan in advance to add adequate staff for the unit.

Reduce Demand for Inpatient Beds

If the inpatient bed is the bottleneck, another way to elevate the bottleneck is by reducing demand for inpatient beds. We have already discussed reducing demand by transferring stable, new admissions to another hospital in the same healthcare system rather than boarding them in the ED. Another option—provided that the ED is large enough and is staffed robustly—would be to temporarily use a section of the ED as an observation or clinical decision unit. Instead of admitting these patients or configuring a new observation unit, patients could wait in this area until a determination about their admission has been made. It is key, however, that such a unit be considered temporary! If it turns out that this strategy is being employed frequently and effectively, the hospital may want to consider investing in a formal observation unit or clinical decision unit.

Many patients who need monitoring or more definitive testing that cannot be completed in the ED may be admitted to the hospital for relatively short stays—for example, patients with low-risk chest pain. Instead of taking up valuable bed space on inpatient units, these patients could be referred out to primary care or cardiology practices that offer onsite stress testing. The practices could have appointments available every day or every other day specifically for ED referrals; the ED's patient volumes would need to be high enough to guarantee that the open slots will be filled. Under the new workflow, a patient with low-risk chest pain who arrives at the ED could be treated in the ED by a rapid rule-out protocol and then discharged with an appointment for an outpatient stress test the next day. The hospital must invest in additional resources such as care management to institute close, reliable follow-up for any patient it discharges in this manner, and it may need to reimburse the primary care or cardiology practice groups for no-shows. Similar arrangements could be made for other testing, including outpatient echocardiograms, magnetic resonance imaging (MRI) scans, or Holter monitors. Likewise, the hospital may need to hire additional staff to accommodate the increase in referrals for testing.

A subset of patients who present to the ED with undifferentiated chest pain, syncope, altered mental status, or abdominal pain traditionally have high rates of admission. However, there is evidence that these admissions neither yield a specific diagnosis nor change patient outcomes. It is possible to safely send many of these

ED patients home instead of admitting them to inpatient beds. Doing so would further reduce demand for inpatient beds, but it would require hospitals to invest in additional care coordination resources to ensure these more complex patients are discharged safely. Elements of a complex ED discharge include providing more education for patients and families; closely following up on patients; and scheduling home health visits, advanced-practice paramedic visits, telemedicine appointments, or telephone checks as needed.

Admission rates typically vary among providers, even within the same ED. Differences in admission rates may be particularly pronounced for specific diagnoses such as congestive heart failure or chronic obstructive pulmonary disease. Reducing this variability will likely translate into better care—a principle that also appears in Six Sigma—and will further reduce demand for inpatient beds through more robust discharge practices. Physician groups could invest resources into developing treatment algorithms and admission and discharge criteria, based on best practices in the literature and within their own group.

Much of the demand for inpatient beds comes from patients who do not need the high level of care provided by the hospital but are not well enough to return to living independently. The best solution is to place these patients in skilled nursing or assisted living facilities, but these facilities typically have long wait lists, especially for patients who are uninsured or underinsured. Patients often remain in the hospital for weeks or months until beds in skilled nursing or assisted living facilities open up. To reduce the demand for inpatient beds, one effective strategy is for the hospital to lease beds from a skilled nursing facility. The hospital pays for the bed until government funding (e.g. Medicaid) kicks in, and then the hospital's lease transfers to another bed for a new patient. Some hospitals are entering into joint ventures with skilled nursing or assisted living facilities, and maintaining part ownership of these beds ensures adequate availability for their patients.

Add Capacity to ED Beds

A hospital's bottleneck resource may be an ED bed rather than an inpatient bed. If so, we can still apply many of the strategies we discussed to elevate the bottleneck of an inpatient bed. For example, we could add capacity by building more rooms in the ED; however, expanding the ED has the same risks and limitations as adding rooms to inpatient units. Although an ED may eventually become too small to adequately support patient volumes (an ED should typically have at least one bed for every 1,500 patients seen annually), expansion is almost certainly not the first step. There are plenty of other measures that can be implemented more quickly.

Compared to inpatient units, it is much easier to add functional capacity to the ED by seeing patients in nontraditional locations: An ED can line its hallways with gurneys or set up an area of chairs to accommodate patients—assuming there is a place to take the patient temporarily while conducting an interview and examination in private. We know of one ED group that, when patient volumes are high, takes over the hospital cafeteria after closing and turns it into an ED annex. Another ED moves its pediatric ED volume to a short stay unit once the short stay unit has closed. During extremely busy influenza seasons or in times of disaster, hospitals frequently set up tents in their parking lots or rent mobile homes and trailers, using cots in lieu of gurneys. Some ED rooms are equipped with double oxygen and air outlets so that a single room can accommodate two patients if needed.

Reduce Demand for ED Beds

While it is easier to temporarily add bottleneck capacity to an ED than to an inpatient unit, it is more difficult to reduce demand. For most patients, the ED is the front door of the hospital—the tip of the spear. The ED can reduce demand by going on ambulance diversion, but when the ED is closed to ambulance traffic it is not available to care for the sickest patients in the community. Diversion forces patients to travel longer distances for emergency care and shifts the burden of volume to other EDs in the area that remain open. Eventually, the shift in ambulance traffic can negatively impact flow in other EDs, forcing them to go on ambulance diversion as well, and then these patients end up back in your ED. Ambulance diversion is also an ineffective way to reduce demand, because ambulances make up a minority of an ED's volume. The majority of ED patients are walk-ins: These patients are unaffected by ambulance diversion and their access to the ED is guaranteed by law.

A better way to reduce demand in the ED is to provide more comprehensive community services, such as increased access to primary care (e.g., same-day appointments, walk-in hours), home health visits, and telemedicine. Unfortunately, such measures require coordinated investment that is often beyond the control of the ED or even the hospital.

Many healthcare systems have opened urgent care clinics near the hospital to help offload demand among lower-acuity patients. Some hospitals have urgent care clinics embedded in or adjacent to their EDs and will triage patients to urgent care beds instead of ED beds, thereby reducing demand.

Perhaps the greatest source of frustration related to ED beds is the practice of boarding patients who have mental health and substance abuse issues. Although these patients do not represent the greatest absolute number of ED patients, they typically have the longest lengths of stay—days or even weeks. Inpatient mental health resources or residential drug and alcohol programs are woefully scarce, and

EDs may not be equipped to offer the appropriate level of treatment. As a result, the entire experience is suboptimal, for both patients and ED staff. Improved wraparound services readily available in the community, such as mental health counseling and substance abuse treatment centers, can prevent patients from needing the ED in the first place. Unfortunately, these solutions are also costly and largely outside the control of the ED and the hospital.

In the city where I (Chris) practice, four health systems have combined resources to open a dedicated mental health hospital, complete with adolescent and emergency psychiatric services. The hospitals elevated the bottlenecks in their EDs by identifying a common need and investing in additional capacity for a specific population. Patients can access the mental health hospital by walking in to the psychiatric ED, via transportation by ambulance, and as transfers from outside hospitals. Mental health patients receive specialized care, and the mental health hospital reduces demand on the other EDs in the area. In my ED, we are not seeing nearly as many mental health patients boarding for days and weeks.

Let's return to the case study from chapter 1 (adapted from Han et al. 2007).

CASE STUDY

An urban, academic Level 1 trauma center with 45,000 annual visits underwent a major expansion to increase the size of its ED from 28 to 53 licensed beds. The expectation was that the expansion would cause ambulance diversion times to decrease, but when the hospital studied the effects of the expansion on ED flow, it found no significant change in ambulance diversion times, the number of episodes of ambulance diversion, or the duration of each episode. Moreover, both the total ED length of stay and the length of stay for boarded patients in the ED increased after the expansion.

What happened?

After reviewing the case study, it may seem as though expanding the ED was a way for the hospital to elevate the bottleneck—but since we don't understand the hospital's true bottleneck, we don't know whether this perception is accurate. The hospital assumed (as many readers likely will) that the bottleneck was an ED bed. As we now know, if the bottleneck was incorrectly identified, then the hospital expanded capacity of a nonbottleneck which, by definition, already had more than sufficient capacity. An hour saved on a nonbottleneck is a mirage that does not add to productivity. The hospital invested in increasing bottleneck capacity, but the expansion moved the hospital away from its goal. This outcome suggests that either the hospital did not *first* optimize flow through the bottleneck (if the

ED bed is the bottleneck) or that the true bottleneck for the hospital lies *outside* of the ED (in which case a lot of money was spent to elevate a nonbottleneck).

Regardless of where the bottleneck resides, the overarching reason the expansion was unsuccessful is that the hospital didn't follow the 5FS. Leadership jumped to the fourth focusing step (elevate the bottleneck) instead of beginning with the first focusing step (identify the bottleneck). If the hospital had identified the bottleneck, and it was not the ED bed, we would already know why the project was unsuccessful. If the hospital correctly assumed that the ED bed was in fact the bottleneck, it should have executed focusing steps two and three, exploiting and subordinating to the bottleneck. In our analysis of this case study from chapter 1, we learned that the hospital did not change the process by which patients were managed, so throughput did not increase. If the hospital had followed the second and especially third focusing steps, it would have had the opportunity to implement changes to patient management. By skipping straight to the fourth focusing step, the hospital set itself up for an ineffective expansion that did not improve patient flow. Essentially, the hospital built a bigger sink without first fixing the clog.

Coincidentally, the hospital from our bonus case study in chapter 4 is also undergoing an expansion. Despite all the work its leaders put into subordination, the ED continues to have flow problems—it is simply too small. Hospital leadership has every reason to be confident that their new, larger department will be successful, however, because they spent time identifying their bottleneck, exploiting their bottleneck, and subordinating to their bottleneck. They are now ready to elevate their bottleneck!

SUMMARY

- If the bottleneck remains after exploitation and subordination, it is time to elevate the bottleneck.
- Elevating the bottleneck means adding capacity to or reducing demand for the bottleneck, usually by making an investment.
- The ultimate goal of elevating the bottleneck is to turn it into a nonbottleneck.

REFERENCE

Han, J. H., Z. Chuan, D. J. France, S. Zhong, I. Jones, A. B. Storrow, and D. Aronsky. 2007. "The Effect of Emergency Department Expansion on Emergency Department Overcrowding." *Academic Emergency Medicine* 14 (4): 338–43.

CHAPTER 6

The Fifth Focusing Step:
If the Bottleneck Has Been
Broken, Go Back to Step One

OBJECTIVES

- Recognize the importance of constantly searching for new bottlenecks
- Learn to overcome inertia
- Understand TOC as a process of continuous improvement

AFTER SUCCESSFULLY WORKING through the preceding four focusing steps, we should begin to see tangible improvements in patient flow throughout a hospital. It may even seem as though the original bottleneck is no longer a problem. Keep in mind that there will always be a bottleneck. Bottlenecks are not inherently bad; they are a part of any system—the cost of doing business. If your hospital had no bottlenecks, it would be caring for an infinite number of patients and employing an infinite number of resources, all with unlimited capacity. If this does describe your hospital, are you hiring?

At some point, you will break the bottleneck that you identified in the first focusing step, but the work doesn't stop. TOC is an *ongoing process of continuous improvement.* You need to find the new bottleneck, and that's what the fifth focusing step is all about.

If the bottleneck has been broken, go back to the first focusing step and identify the new bottleneck. Don't let inertia be the new bottleneck! In the fifth focusing step, decisions that were previously made to exploit, subordinate to, and elevate the bottleneck may need to be adjusted for a new bottleneck.

With each iteration of the 5FS, we will identify new bottlenecks and new ways to exploit, subordinate, and elevate them. As a result, each subsequent iteration of the 5FS has the potential to be more challenging or yield less dramatic results than previous iterations—we achieved most of the easy wins when we broke the first bottleneck. Fortunately, during subsequent iterations, everyone involved will be more experienced, and their ability to apply TOC will be more sophisticated.

It is important to understand that, without vigilance and ongoing effort, workflow reverts back to the old ways and all gains in flow improvements will be lost. Hospitals typically have a fair amount of turnover, and it does not take long for culture to regress and silos to reappear. For flow improvements to continue, a hospital needs a dedicated team and dedicated leader, ongoing support from hospital leadership, and ongoing investment of time and resources. Moreover, new processes, policies, and procedures must be embedded into the culture of the hospital; otherwise, the hospital risks losing gains as legacy changes are forgotten.

Fortunately, just when employees begin to feel complacent or lose interest, we can stop playing defense and start playing offense. The real fun begins! In subsequent chapters we will discuss constraints (a concept we brought up, then asked you to forget, in the introduction). A constraint is a resource around which we synchronize all of our system's activities and resources—similar, but not identical, to a bottleneck—to achieve even greater gains in productivity. The constraint may or may not be the bottleneck, but regardless, it helps us make strategic decisions about the "release of products" in clinics, outpatient settings, and possibly emergency and surgical departments as well. A constraint also helps us make smart decisions about staff hiring and cuts, expanding existing services, and developing new service lines.

Right now, you may think that you have bottlenecks everywhere and that your hospital flow is not only unmanageable but also unfixable—absolutely not true! You may barely have the bandwidth to *react* to all the flow problems in your hospital and cannot believe that being *proactive* is a possibility—it will be! If you use TOC, you will be able to stop running around putting out fires (we call this "expediting," and it isn't good). You will be able to plan for surges in volume, take care of more patients, provide better quality care, and improve staff satisfaction. Honest.

Let's look at a case study where inertia has become the new bottleneck.

CASE STUDY

A medium-sized community ED has an average annual census of 40,000 visits and sees primarily low- to moderate-acuity patients. Its wait times began to increase, and the hospital flow committee traced the increase to a scarcity of available ED beds. To address this issue, the ED created a fast track that operates

(continued)

between 8:00 a.m. and 10:00 p.m. every day. Lower-acuity patients are triaged to the fast track, where physician assistants evaluate and treat them in a converted hallway lined with chairs. There is a single gurney, partitioned off for privacy, to facilitate the occasional examination that can't be performed in a chair. When the fast track was initially implemented, wait times in the ED improved dramatically. More recently, three urgent care centers have opened within a short drive of the ED.

Why did the fast track reduce wait times initially? What ED patient characteristics support the decision to open a fast track? How will ED wait times change (if at all) now that urgent care centers have opened in the area?

How will the fifth focusing step help answer these questions? What will happen if inertia becomes the new bottleneck?

When the fast track opened, wait times for the ED improved because the fast track acted as a parallel workflow for patients who did not need the bottleneck resource (an ED bed). Before the fast track opened, patients with ankle sprains or colds might wait hours for an available ED bed, even though they didn't need a bed for their visit. Once the fast track became available, low-acuity patients no longer had to wait behind the bottleneck. They only had to wait until another low-acuity patient had been treated and discharged, which could reduce their lengths of stays from hours to minutes. Fast tracks, ambulatory care units, and PIT models work best when an ED consistently has so many low-acuity patients that they compete with sicker, more complicated patients for ED beds.

A problem develops when the population of low-acuity patients shrinks. If there is no longer a sufficient number of patients to support a fast track, then much of the fast track area sits empty. The population of sicker ED patients presumably remains the same, but now a portion of usable ED space that could be used to treat sicker patients is sitting empty in the fast track area. In other words, the bottleneck is not being exploited.

When urgent care centers open near a hospital, they compete with the hospital's ED for low-acuity patients. ED volumes decrease as low-acuity patients realize that urgent care centers are a cheaper, more convenient option. If the ED doesn't respond to the erosion of low-acuity volumes—potentially by reducing or closing the fast track area—then overall flow will likely become worse than before the fast track area opened.

The fifth focusing step asks us to recognize the dynamics that result from breaking the bottleneck. It is implicit in the fifth focusing step that decisions previously made to exploit, subordinate, and elevate an initial bottleneck may need to be modified to adjust to a new bottleneck. You continually revisit your prior work so that inertia does not become your new bottleneck. Otherwise, you will inevitably backslide, which compromises competitiveness, staff wellness, and patient care.

SUMMARY

- TOC is a process of continuous improvement.
- There will always be a bottleneck; when you break a bottleneck, you must look for the next one.
- Decisions made to exploit and subordinate a previous bottleneck may need to be adjusted for a new bottleneck.
- Don't let inertia become the new bottleneck.

PART II

Moving Beyond the Bottleneck: Constraint Management in the Emergency Department and Inpatient Units

I (CHRIS) AM NOT a big guy, and I have a disinclination toward being pummeled. It's no surprise that my football experience consists of a few flag football games in fifth grade gym class, some epic Super Bowl commercials, a medical school roommate who armchair-quarterbacked three years of Alabama–Tennessee games, and every episode of *Friday Night Lights*. Nonetheless, I think I'm on firm ground when I use the following football analogy.

A busy hospital is like the line of scrimmage just after the ball has been snapped—a panoply of bodies crashing into each other. The defensive line struggles to get to the quarterback, but no matter how hard the defensive players push, they rarely seem to make progress. The quarterback doesn't usually get sacked, and the line of scrimmage hardly ever gets pushed back. I think of a hospital with poor flow in much the same way. Inpatient units are full of patients ready for discharge with no place to go. EDs—closed to ambulances but with a steady stream of walk-ins clamoring for attention—have packed waiting rooms and fully occupied gurneys lining the hallways. Hospital staff struggle as they fight to move patients through the system. The comparison to football may be a bit melodramatic, but it illustrates the concept of *playing defense*.

When we first consider improving patient flow, we're playing defense. We look for any resource or tool that will give us an advantage or bring order to the chaos. Identifying bottlenecks, for example, is playing defense. It's how we start turning chaos into some semblance of order.

When small wins become bigger wins, when we start to break the gridlock, when we begin to smash bottlenecks and open up pathways, we stand to gain a lot of ground. Then it's time to *play offense*! That's what the second part of this book is about.

In the opening chapters of *The Goal*, Eli Goldratt describes a factory with horrible flow problems. It is almost impossible to navigate the factory floor because it is cluttered with giant piles of inventory. The floor is so crowded that it's hard to get a handle on the nature of the factory's problems. By working the 5FS to identify and clear the bottleneck, the piles of inventory disappear. As soon as the factory floor is easier to navigate, the road to further productivity becomes much clearer.

At this point in the novel, the characters stop focusing on the system's bottleneck and begin to focus on the system's *constraint*. Like those piles of inventory on the factory floor (or those piles of bodies on the football field), when we first start looking at flow, we see a pile of patients that blocks our ability to find a clear path through the system. After smashing bottlenecks and improving flow, work feels easier, and we should have enough clarity to think more strategically. We are ready to play offense.

To understand how to play offense, you need to know what a constraint is and how it differs from a bottleneck.

CHAPTER 7

Understanding a Constraint

OBJECTIVES

- Understand the definition of a constraint
- Introduce constraint management
- Know how a constraint differs from a bottleneck
- Begin to learn how to identify a constraint

THE CONSTRAINT IS the resource in the system that we select to determine the system's output. As with a bottleneck, what the constraint produces in an hour is what the system produces in an hour. The constraint is typically the predominant resource in the system. It is usually the most complex, critical, or expensive resource; it has the most touch points and is often the most difficult to replace. Unlike a bottleneck, however, *the constraint serves as a focus around which we coordinate all of the system's other resources and activities.* This approach, which we will refer to in this book as constraint management, is a huge departure from current business practices where siloed mentality is the norm.

You are familiar with the concept of improving flow by applying the 5FS to a system. We now need to reframe the 5FS in terms of the constraint:

Step 1: Identify the system's constraint
Step 2: Decide how to exploit the system's constraint
Step 3: Subordinate everything else to the decisions made in Step 2
Step 4: Elevate the system's constraint
Step 5: If a system's constraint has changed, go back to step 1. Don't let inertia be the new constraint.

IDENTIFYING THE CONSTRAINT

When I (Chris) was in the ninth grade, I was invited to the Hollywood Bowl by my friend Karl. Zubin Mehta was conducting the Los Angeles Philharmonic Orchestra; it must have been one of his last performances as music director. I knew virtually nothing about classical music. My only prior experience with a conductor was Mickey Mouse as the Sorcerer's Apprentice in the film *Fantasia*. Mickey had no clue what he was doing, and he drove the system into chaos—good movie, great actor, lousy conductor. Until that concert, I thought that the musicians played their instruments and the music somehow came together. I took for granted the importance of the conductor, who is responsible for synchronizing the musicians, setting the rhythm, and bringing many elements together to create a single, magical, cohesive piece of music. As Mickey learned, if the constraint isn't optimized, the system flounders.

Similar to an orchestra making music, hospital flow requires coordination between many different elements, and the constraint is the resource around which the elements are synchronized. Specifically, when managing a constraint, all of the system's activities are synchronized around the *pace* of the constraint. Moreover, since the constraint resource is the conductor of the entire system, it is important to make sure you have identified the constraint correctly: Does it make sense to organize all of your system's activities around the resource that you have identified as the constraint? If not, then you have chosen incorrectly.

Let's return to the Mattel factory example to see how the constraint works. The factory had fewer right arms for Barbie dolls than it had all other parts, and we determined that the right arm was the bottleneck. With the right arm as the bottleneck, the 5FS can be used to implement changes to break the bottleneck, allowing all the Barbie doll orders to be filled. But what if we made the right-armed Barbies the *constraint*? As we work through the 5FS, this time treating the right arm as the constraint rather than the bottleneck, we see that the factory would increase the capacity of the right-arm station to make more dolls. As long as there were enough right arms, Barbie production would continue to increase. All of the factory's activities would be driven by the productivity or pace of the right-arm station. In the fourth focusing step, the factory would invest in increasing capacity at the right-arm station, buy increasingly more right arms, invest in the nonconstraint resources so that they could keep up with right arm production, and produce an unlimited number of Barbie dolls—regardless of whether or not Mattel would be able to sell them.

That's why it doesn't make sense to use the right arm as the constraint. The thought exercise tells us that we probably selected the wrong resource to synchronize the system's activities. As a bottleneck, the right arm *limits* how many dolls the factory can produce, but it should not *dictate* how many dolls are produced. Therefore, the right arm should not be the constraint. The factory's constraint is the resource that best determines how many Barbie dolls the factory needs to make and in what period of time.

For the Mattel factory—and for a retail model in general—the marketplace is the constraint.[1] Here's the reason: If the Mattel factory has an order for a certain number of dolls, it wants to produce that number of dolls. The factory doesn't want to produce more dolls than it can sell. Dolls that are made but not sold count as inventory, not throughput, so simply making more dolls is a nonproductive move that will cost that factory money. Instead, the factory should focus on making the appropriate number of dolls but improving workflow so that making dolls can be faster, more reliable, more predictable, and less costly. Doing so keeps current customers happy and gives the factory a competitive advantage over other factories with respect to getting more customers. The market is the constraint, and, as such, the activities of the Mattel factory are synchronized to the market demand for Barbies. When Mattel attracts more customers, demand grows, which increases the constraint's capacity. Through a process of ongoing improvement, the factory continues to refine its workflow to meet the increase in demand, which helps further increase market share—and the cycle continues. When we select the marketplace as the constraint, we are effectively coordinating all resources around the constraint to guard against making too few or too many dolls.

That's fine for making Barbie dolls—now let's talk about healthcare. In the following chapters, we are going to look at some patient flow case studies to demonstrate how the concept of the constraint works for our specific purposes. We will apply constraint management to an ED and an inpatient unit. Later in the book, we will discuss constraint management in an outpatient setting. Before we can dive in, however, we need to introduce and discuss a few new concepts.[2] These concepts are indispensable tools for exploiting and subordinating to the constraint.

SUMMARY

- The constraint is the resource in the system that we select to determine the system's output.
- All of the system's other resources are coordinated around the constraint.
- The constraint is typically the predominant resource in the system. It is usually the most complex, critical, and expensive resource; it has the most touch points and is often the most difficult to replace.
- After selecting the constraint, reframe the 5FS in terms of the constraint.

NOTES

1. In the TOC community, there is some debate as to whether or not this statement is actually true. A purist would say that the marketplace would be the constraint only if you controlled 100 percent of the market and if there weren't any additional customers for your product. In this book, when we refer to the market as the constraint, what we mean is that whoever in your organization is responsible for attracting more customers or increasing market share is actually the new constraint. With sales as the constraint, a system should then subordinate to the sales function by producing only what the sales department can sell. In a hospital, clinic, or healthcare system, when we say that the market has become the constraint, what we mean is that clinical operations within the system no longer control the pace. The pace is controlled by the factor(s) responsible for increasing patient volume (e.g., the advertising and marketing department, a community outreach program working to increase referral patterns, the CEO hiring away a transplant surgery program from another hospital to increase high-profile surgical cases). Although we will refer to this constraint as the marketplace, it is, in fact, a proxy.

2. Because these concepts are so important, and to make things easier for readers who don't need to learn about both inpatient and outpatient systems, we will review the tools again in our discussion of the outpatient setting. That way, you won't have to read through chapters that aren't relevant to your specific needs.

CHAPTER 8

More Arrows in the Quiver: Additional Concepts in the Theory of Constraints

---

OBJECTIVES

- Understand Drum Buffer Rope as a scheduling system
- Understand different types of buffers and how to use them to protect the constraint
- Learn full kitting and its importance in constraint management
- Apply Value Stream Mapping to improve the constraint's productivity

---

TOC IS MUCH more than the 5FS. Since the publication of *The Goal*, more tools have been developed in many subjects, including operations management, supply chain management, project management, decision making, strategic planning, leadership skills, marketing, and sales. While we are certain that the rest of the TOC body of knowledge can be applied to healthcare management, for the purpose of this book, we will introduce only a few additional concepts that directly apply to patient flow.

DRUM BUFFER ROPE

We established in earlier chapters that we want to minimize works-in-process (i.e., inventory) to improve a system's performance. Constraint management accomplishes this by synchronizing resources around the constraint so that there are not more materials or products released into the system than the constraint can handle. If too much is released, we have to continually play defense. If too little is released, however, the constraint is starved—it runs out of things to do and sits idle.

At the Mattel factory, for example, the system produces only as many dolls as the right-arm station produces. There's no need to release more materials into the system than the right-arm station can handle. In fact, if we have left-armed Barbie dolls piling up behind the right-arm station and we don't stop releasing new materials—torsos, legs, and left arms—then we will create ever-larger reserves of inventory: unfinished dolls that will pile up all over the factory floor. We'll have to continually play defense to gain control over the chaos in the system. Conversely, any problem in production upstream of the constraint can cause a delay in feeding parts to the constraint. If the constraint runs out of work, then it sits idle and is not being exploited.

Drum Buffer Rope (DBR) is a methodology that provides the framework in constraint management for scheduling when, and how much, new work should be introduced into a system. It was first introduced by Eliyahu Goldratt in a follow-up book, *The Race* (Goldratt and Cox 1986). DBR is a scheduling process focused on improving flow by limiting the release of raw materials into a system to support a selected critical resource. DBR synchronizes all the resources or activities in the system; it tells us how many materials or products the constraint can handle, when the constraint is ready for more, how to avoid releasing too much, and how to release enough to protect the constraint from ever running out of work, even if there is glitch at a non-constraint resource.

At the Mattel factory, DBR would tell us when to introduce a new torso to the factory floor and start turning it into a completed doll. DBR is a way to signal to the other resources that the constraint is ready for more work. DBR also ensures that the system could continue production even if the constraint starts to run out of materials and additional materials are unexpectedly delayed.

The Drum

The *drum* in DBR signals the pace of the constraint. Have you seen pictures of American colonists marching into battle against the British during the American Revolution? There is always a drummer who played while the soldiers marched to the beat. The drum set the pace for the entire unit and synchronized every soldier's steps to that pace. In short, the drum kept the unit of soldiers together. In DBR, the drum "beats" at the pace of the constraint. If the constraint speeds up or slows down, then the drum changes the beat accordingly. The drum signals to the system that it's time to release new product. In the Mattel factory, we determined that the marketplace is the constraint—so the drum is the pace of the marketplace. It determines how many dolls customers need. If the factory needs to fill an order for 1,000 dolls, and the order is due in 10 days, then 1,000 dolls in 10 days is the pace. Enough parts must be released into the factory to fill the order within the set amount of time. If the market demand increases and the factory needs to fill more orders, the drum signals to release more parts.

The Rope

While the drum signals the pace of the system, the *rope* ties the release of new materials to the drum. For our purpose, the rope can be a computerized or manual signal controlling the time of the release of materials. In the Mattel factory, suppose the materials planner is responsible not only for ensuring that there are enough parts to fill the order in time—1,000 Barbie dolls in 10 days—but also for making sure that cash isn't tied up in excess inventory that isn't needed or can't be sold. The materials planner (using the rope signal) acts as the mechanism for releasing material with enough time so that the constraint won't run out of work and the order will be delivered by the promised delivery date. The rope also prevents releasing material too early, which could result in inventory increasing beyond what the constraint can handle.

The Buffer

Any system has inevitable variations in activities and resources, and because unexpected delays in production are inevitable, we need to build safety into the system. In DBR, the *buffer* helps protect the constraint from running out of work and becoming idle. Suppose the Mattel factory needs to produce 1,000 Barbie dolls to satisfy the market. Also, let's assume that if everything is perfect, completing that order will take two days. The reality is that due to expected variability, it would not be wise to release the materials two days before they are needed. People can be absent, quality problems can occur, and machines can break down. We need to release the material with enough extra time built in (in case of unexpected problems or delays) that the dolls will still reach the constraint (the market) on time. At the same time, we do not want to release the order too early, which could increase works-in-process to the point that the factory becomes chaotic (after all, there may be other orders on the floor competing for resources). The time between when the parts are released to the floor and when they are needed is the buffer. In this case, we are using a time buffer—illustrated in the factory example.

Exhibit 8.1 is a graphic representation of the DBR model in the Mattel factory.

Similarly, if you need to make 1,000 Barbie dolls, you would not just order exactly 1,000 of each doll part. An employee who is responsible for attaching the

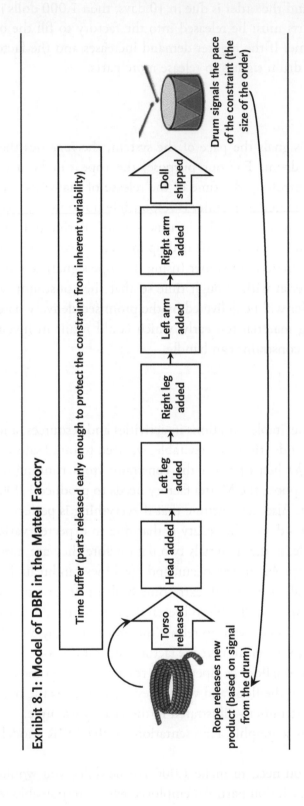

Exhibit 8.1: Model of DBR in the Mattel Factory

head to the torso might accidentally drop one of the heads down a drainpipe—gone forever. If the factory has only 1,000 parts in inventory, then the unexpected loss of a part will prevent the factory from filling the order on time, since the replacement part will take a while to order. Therefore, the factory must order some excess of each part to protect against variability and unexpected problems—the total amount of inventory including the excess parts constitutes a stock buffer.

DBR in the Real World

Initially, it can be difficult to understand how DBR applies to real-world scenarios. What better way to learn how the real world works than by watching *I Love Lucy*? In one of *I Love Lucy's* quintessential episodes, Lucy and Ethel get jobs at a candy factory. It's hilarious—and educational, if you're looking for an excellent tutorial on DBR.

In the episode, Lucy and Ethel work on an assembly line in a candy factory. Pieces of candy are placed onto a conveyor belt upstream of Lucy and Ethel, somewhere off-camera. As the candy travels toward them, their job is to wrap each piece and place it back on the conveyor belt. The candy then travels downstream, presumably to be boxed and shipped. Can you identify the drum, buffer, and rope in this scenario?

Lucy and Ethel are the constraint. The system *should* be synchronized to them. The drum is their pace—how quickly they can wrap the candy. The release of candy onto the conveyor belt is the rope (which clearly was not executed well, as the video shows!). The conveyor belt physically ties the release of new materials to the drum by releasing product (unwrapped candy) into the system. The drum should release new materials according to how quickly Lucy and Ethel can work. Instead of releasing one piece of candy at a time, waiting for Lucy and Ethel to wrap the candy, and then releasing the next piece, the conveyor belt is lined with a steady stream of candy. As one piece of candy gets wrapped, there are several more pieces lined up behind it on the belt. These pieces are placed on the conveyor belt earlier than needed to protect Lucy and Ethel from running out of candy and therefore sitting idle. The buffer is the time between when a piece of candy is placed on the conveyor belt and when Lucy and Ethel are ready for the piece of candy. As Lucy and Ethel gain more experience and get faster at wrapping candy, the time buffer should be reduced. In that case, the rope mechanism should be adjusted to bring candy down the conveyor belt more quickly. Conversely, if Lucy and Ethel start to slow down, then the rope should adjust to bring them candy more slowly.

One of the greatest parts of this scene is what happens when too much product is released. As the conveyor belt moves along, a few pieces of unwrapped candy get away from Lucy and Ethel. They know they'll be fired if they miss any candy, so they start to grab the unwrapped pieces from the belt. Soon there is a pile of unwrapped candy in front of them. When the supervisor comes to check up on them, Lucy and Ethel hide the stash of candy by stuffing it in their mouths, in their hats, and down their shirts. When the supervisor sees how well they seem to be doing, she screams out, "Speed it up!" and the conveyor belt starts to move double time. Hilarious!

BUFFER MANAGEMENT

Buffers not only protect the constraint from inherent variations or unexpected problems in the system, but also provide visual cues to coordinate and improve the system's activities. By tracking how buffers are used up and replenished, we can gather information to set priorities. We can also identify when and where we might need to step in and solve problems and see what activities or resources create most of the delays. We use all of this information to make targeted improvements. As we will discuss in later chapters, Buffer Management is a critical TOC tool for managing flow in inpatient units.

An Example of Buffer Management

We've established that the constraint resource needs to work on new materials or it sits idle. For the sake of simplicity, imagine a scenario where the constraint works on one piece of material at a time. If the system has no buffer, then a single piece of material is delivered to the constraint exactly when the constraint is ready for it. The constraint processes the piece of material, sends it downstream, and works on the next piece of material, which shows up exactly when the constraint needs it. There is, literally, no time to spare. As long as the next piece of material is available to the constraint at exactly the right time, the system works—but in reality, it's virtually impossible to perfectly balance a system in this manner. If the constraint speeds up, it will be ready for the next piece of material sooner than usual, but the next piece of material may not be ready for the constraint. There could be a glitch in one of the upstream events that prepares new material for the constraint. Eventually, some event will occur that delays the process—it's inevitable—and the constraint will sit idle. Buffers protect the constraint by making sure that the next piece of material is delivered a little bit sooner than when the constraint needs it. A buffer protects the constraint in the event that either the constraint is early or the next piece of material is delayed. It's pretty easy to see how a buffer can pro-tect the constraint, but it's more complicated to understand how the buffer helps coordinate activities throughout the system.

Let's look at an example to illustrate the principles of Buffer Management. Imagine that it's tax season and that Joe is the only certified public accountant (CPA) at Joe's Accounting. Joe is the constraint resource. He should always have a tax return to work on, because if he sits idle while there are still tax returns to complete, he won't be able to file his clients' returns on time. Joe wants a buffer of six tax returns at any given time. If he has fewer than six returns, he may run out—perhaps some of the tax returns are unexpectedly easy to complete, for example; if he has more than six returns on his desk, he feels overwhelmed and becomes inefficient.

When Joe has six tax returns on his desk, the buffer is sufficient and does not need replenishment. As Joe works through the returns—known as buffer consumption—he will need more files added to the pile. By tracking buffer consumption, Joe's staff knows when to bring him more returns.

TOC divides the buffer into thirds and assigns each segment a color based on its level of consumption. The color is a quick visual cue that easily signals Joe's progress to everyone in the office. When Joe has worked his way through 0–33 percent of the buffer, the buffer is in the green third. When 34–66 percent has been consumed, the buffer is in the yellow third. The buffer is in the red third at 67–100 percent consumption. Color-coded buffer consumption can be represented graphically (exhibit 8.2).

When Joe has run out of tax returns, the buffer has been fully consumed, indicated by the color black. The signal can be deployed simply: Joe's staff can place a green card on top of a pile of six returns, a yellow card one-third of the way down (between the second and third returns), a red card two-thirds of the way down (between the fourth and fifth returns), and a black card under the pile. When Joe begins, he places the green card on the edge of his desk so his staff can easily see it. When he finishes one-third of the buffer, he places the yellow card on his desk. When he finishes two-thirds of the buffer, he places the red card on his desk. When he finishes his last return, he places the black card on his desk.

Exhibit 8.2: Buffer Consumption, Divided into Thirds

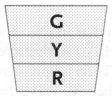

To track buffer consumption, we divide the buffer into thirds.
G, Y, and R (green, yellow, and red, respectively) represent buffer consumption:
G = 0–33%, Y = 34–66%, R = 67–100%.

Alex, Joe's office manager, is responsible for making sure that Joe never runs out of returns. As soon as Joe puts the yellow card on his desk, Alex should bring Joe two new returns.

This plan works well for Joe and his team—unless Alex isn't around to replenish the buffer by delivering new tax returns. If there are instances when the plan doesn't work, then a backup plan is necessary. If the buffer turns from green to yellow while Alex isn't around, Joe's team needs to devise a backup plan for replenishing the buffer. The backup plan could be that Rich will go look for Alex, Lisa will grab files from the inbox and bring them to Joe, and Rory will look for new tax returns in the morning mail. If Joe consumes two-thirds of the buffer and places the red card on his desk, the office must then execute the backup plan.

There should not be much of a disruption in flow, even when the buffer turns red; the office is ready with their plan and should have time to carry it out in an orderly manner before Joe works through the remaining files. However, in the event that the backup plan does not work as hoped and Joe consumes the entire buffer, he will place the black card on his desk, and everyone in the office will need to drop whatever they're doing and figure out how to get Joe more tax returns—this is called expediting, and it is very disruptive.

Benefits of Buffers

Subdividing the buffer helps prioritize all the activities in the system. When one-third of a buffer has been consumed (the yellow card), the system's priority is to create a backup plan. When two-thirds of a buffer has been consumed (the red card), the priority is to execute the backup plan. When the buffer has been fully consumed (the black card), the priority is to expedite by stopping all other activities to work on the buffer. In healthcare, a buffer could be having patients arrive early for their appointments to complete paperwork and to check their vitals, or scheduling three patients in the same time slot for an outpatient imaging scan.

If a system has multiple buffers, the color coding also indicates which buffer needs attention first. Buffers that have been fully consumed (black) should be replenished first, followed by buffers that are in the red, yellow, and green, in that order.

By measuring buffer consumption, it is also possible to quickly determine where problems in a system originate. If Joe reaches a red or black card, there is a delay upstream of the constraint (Joe). There is a problem in the chain of events that delivers new tax returns to his desk (the series of events that feed the constraint). On the other hand, if Joe rarely gets to the yellow card, that's a sign that new material isn't being processed. There is a problem at the constraint (e.g., Joe lost his glasses), or there is a problem downstream of the constraint that is now inhibiting the constraint.

Finally, buffers help with ongoing process improvement. Buffer consumption can be tracked over time. If a buffer is frequently in the red or black, we can closely examine the events around the buffer to understand why the buffer keeps running out. Once the cause of the problem has been determined, we can reengineer this part of the system to fix it.

FULL KITTING

We have established that the constraint is not being exploited when it sits idle. The same holds true if a constraint is being used ineffectively—in other words, when it spends time on nonconstraint activities. Joe can help us illustrate this principle. As the sole CPA in his firm, Joe is the only person in the office who can prepare tax returns. If Joe is properly exploited as the constraint, then he will spend all of his time on the constraint-appropriate task: preparing tax returns. Nonconstraint tasks, such as tracking down missing files or ordering office supplies, divert Joe's attention away from the constraint activity and so should be done by someone else (i.e., a nonconstraint resource).

In TOC there is a concept called full kitting, which states that no constraint-level task begins unless everything necessary to complete the task is available to the constraint at the outset. For Joe's Accounting, a full kit would be having everything Joe needs to prepare tax returns—organized client files, tax tables, pads of paper, pens—waiting at Joe's desk when he gets into the office. A full kit protects Joe from having to perform nonconstraint tasks, such as getting up and looking for more pens and paper, that can be performed by someone who is not the constraint.

The concept of a full kit is readily applicable to healthcare, and could include

- having a suture kit, local anesthetic, gloves, and suture material available to the physician before repairing a laceration;
- ensuring that the ultrasound probe is clean, gel is available, and the patient is in a gown before starting the scan; or
- making sure that the airway cart is fully stocked with laryngoscopes, blades, endotracheal tubes, and adjuvant airway devices before a patient needs intubation.

VALUE STREAM MAPPING

Value Stream Mapping (VSM) is a Lean tool that identifies wasted steps in a process. We'll present a simplified version of a VSM for our purposes. VSM begins by outlining the flow of information, from the customer to the business and from the business to the parts supplier. The information flow moves from right to left in

VSM. Next, all the steps currently involved in creating product are documented, beginning with raw materials and ending with customer delivery. Called materials flow, this chain of steps moves from left to right in VSM. Finally, inventory is measured at each step, along with how much cash is tied up in inventory and how long each step takes to complete.

Once the relevant information has been collected, it is used to draw a physical map. The map will indicate how much time in the process is being wasted, how much inventory is tied up in waste, and how much the inventory costs. When looking for wasted steps, keep in mind that a value stream map is geared to customer demand. A step that directly benefits the customer is a valuable step, and a step that does not directly benefit the customer is considered waste. For example, the steps that turn raw material into finished product bring value to the customer, but the customer derives no direct value from the time it takes to get raw materials to the factory, the time it takes to repair machinery, the time finished goods sit on the factory floor, or the time the factory sits idle during a lunch break. Every minute in the entire process not spent directly creating product is considered wasted time, because it does not directly add value to the customer.

With these points in mind, we can draw a value stream map of the Mattel factory. In exhibit 8.3, triangles represent inventory, with the dollar amount of inventory onsite in that step of the process designated below each triangle. We can see that information flows from the customer to the factory; based on the customer's needs, the factory orders parts from the supplier. Materials flow from the supplier to the warehouse, where they are stored for 120 hours (five days) before being sent to the factory. In the factory, it takes eight hours to manufacture

Exhibit 8.3: Value Stream Map of Mattel Factory

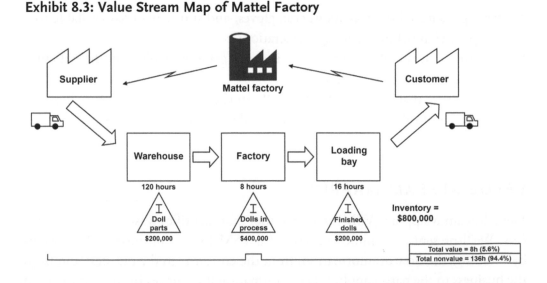

all of the Barbie dolls that can be produced in a day. The completed dolls are then transferred to the loading bay, where they remain until being shipped to the customer 16 hours later (the next day). The factory doesn't make money until the customer receives the dolls, but the factory pays out money to the supplier before the parts are shipped.

The map shows us that at any given time, there is an average of $200,000 of inventory sitting in the warehouse, $400,000 of inventory in various stages of completion sitting in the factory, and $200,000 of finished dolls sitting in the loading bay—a total of $800,000 of inventory. Not only does the $800,000 represent cash tied up in inventory, which negatively impacts cash flow, but it also represents additional expenses, such as financing, rent, labor, equipment, and utility costs, associated with holding the inventory.

The map can also be used to differentiate between steps in the process with value and steps with nonvalue. In this simplified diagram, flow through the entire process is represented by three steps. Since value and nonvalue are determined from the perspective of the customer, the only value steps are those directly involved with producing Barbie dolls. The customer derives no direct value from parts in the warehouse or completed products in the loading bay. The map shows, however, that products spend the vast majority of time in nonvalue steps: In this example, less than 6 percent of the entire process adds value for the customer.

VSM has made it clear that at the Mattel factory, significant cash is tied up in inventory and nonvalue steps. Using exhibit 8.3 as a blueprint, process improvements should focus on shortening or, if possible, eliminating nonvalue steps. The map indicates that trying to eliminate the nonvalue steps will be considerably more productive than trying to shorten the steps that do add value.

ADDING CONTEXT

Now that we have introduced these tools—DBR, Buffer Management, full kitting, and VSM—we can apply them to specific use cases—namely, ED and inpatient unit flow—which we will do in the following chapters. Intimately associated with the 5FS, these tools

- confirm that the selected constraint makes sense (first focusing step),
- help identify ways to exploit the constraint (second focusing step),
- provide a roadmap for subordinating the system's activities to the constraint (third focusing step),
- offer clarity for elevating the constraint (fourth focusing step), and
- aid in developing ongoing process improvement (fifth focusing step).

SUMMARY

- Drum Buffer Rope is a scheduling process focused on improving flow by limiting the release of raw materials into a system to support a selected critical resource. The drum signals the pace of the constraint to the entire system.
- The rope releases new materials based on the pace of the constraint.
- The buffer helps protect the constraint against inevitable variations in activities and resources that can cause the constraint to run out of work and become idle.
- Buffers can be divided into thirds, and colors can be assigned to represent how much of a buffer has been consumed: green for less than one-third buffer consumption, yellow for one-third to two-thirds buffer consumption, red for more than two-thirds consumption, and black for complete consumption of the buffer.
- The buffer's color provides visual cues to coordinate and prioritize everyone's activities.
- Full kit ensures that all the supplies, tools, or information that the constraint needs to complete a task are ready at the outset of the task.
- Value Stream Mapping (VSM) helps identify which steps in a process do not add value, how much time these steps are wasting, how much inventory is tied up in waste, and how much that inventory is costing.
- VSM is geared to customer demand; steps that directly benefit the customer add value and steps that do not directly benefit the customer do not add value.

REFERENCE

Goldratt, E. M., and R. E. Fox. 1986. *The Race.* New York: North River Press.

CHAPTER 9

Using Constraint Management to Improve Emergency Department Flow

---

OBJECTIVES

- Understand the constraint in ED flow
- Examine ED flow through the lens of the 5FS
- Apply DBR and Buffer Management to ED flow
- Augment the emergency physician's productivity through full kitting and VSM
- Create a map of idealized ED flow

WE ESTABLISHED IN THE introduction and chapter 1 that in a hospital, the bottleneck in patient flow is usually outside of the ED and that an hour saved at a nonbottleneck is a mirage. While you might infer that attempts to improve ED flow would therefore not be helpful (since the ED is not usually the bottleneck), hospitals can, in fact, benefit significantly from process improvements to ED flow.

In a typical ED, somewhere between 75–90 percent of patients are discharged from the department. Throughput, the most important of the three operational measurements of TOC, is the rate at which patients are evaluated, treated, and discharged. Therefore, improving throughput for those 75–90 percent of discharged ED patients will directly improve the hospital's overall throughput, even if the ED is not the source of the bottleneck. Improved ED flow will also help ease the burden of inpatient boarding in the ED, along with the resultant morbidity, mortality, and costs. Finally, it will help to reduce ambulance diversion and the number of patients who leave the ED without being seen.

Ultimately, ED flow matters because regardless of how full the hospital is, patients keep coming to the ED. Unlike an inpatient unit, the ED can't close when it's at full capacity. It's legally bound to stay open. Ambulance diversion can deflect a small percentage of patients to other hospitals, but the vast majority of ED patients walk in through the front door.

Considerations for Optimizing Flow

Before we go further, we need to make perfectly clear that in any discussion of patient flow, the *safety of the patients must come first*. Period. Flow theory and operations modeling go out the window when a sick, unstable patient enters the picture. The patient is always the priority. Once the patient has been stabilized, we can go back to optimizing flow.

Also keep in mind the importance of staff wellness. If a change improves workflow but makes an employee's life more difficult, then the change needs to be implemented differently. Changes to workflow should benefit the system *and* its employees: It must be a win-win. Fortunately, improving ED flow allows staff to take better care of patients; employees' jobs will usually feel easier and wellness will then improve.

APPLYING THE 5FS

Step 1: Identify the System's Constraint

Here are a few reminders about constraints: The constraint is the predominant resource in a system; it is the most expensive or complex and has the most touch points. The constraint controls flow through the entire system. All other resources or activities in the system are synchronized to the constraint.

In the ED, the constraint is the ED physician. That's because out of all the staff positions in the department and the resources that interact with patients, the ED physician is the most complex resource. ED physicians have the most training, provide the most specialized care among other ED staff, and are harder to replace—there are fewer board-certified ED physicians nationwide compared to other ED employees (especially in rural areas). The cost per unit of care delivered is higher for physicians than for any other position.

Additionally, ED physicians have the most touch points in patient care. The ED physician is unique in bearing responsibility for all of the ED patients, whereas other employees (e.g., nurses) are responsible only for a subset of patients. The nurse-to-patient ratio in the ED is typically 1:3 or 1:4, whereas the provider-to-patient ratio is usually much higher. Assuming there is more than one nurse in the ED, the ED physician is directly responsible for more patients at any given time than each nurse. Described in terms of throughput, the physician must see every patient in the ED before they can be admitted or discharged.

Although an ED bed may be a bottleneck resource within the department, an ED bed does not make sense as a constraint resource. The pace at which the physician can see patients should dictate the rate at which patients are placed in rooms (in other words, the rate at which product is released into the system). If the bed were the constraint, then the converse would hold true and physicians would see new patients only as quickly (or slowly) as the patients are roomed. However, physicians cannot safely speed up their pace beyond their ability simply because more patients have been roomed. Likewise, physicians should not sit idle simply because all the rooms are full, especially since the physician can see patients elsewhere—in the hallway, on a chair, at triage. Since the flow of patients through the ED is controlled by the constraint, there will inevitably be times when non-constraint resources are idle. From a cost and resource allocation perspective, it's far worse for the physician to sit idle while waiting for a room than for a room to sit idle while waiting for the physician. If the physician sits idle, patients cannot be treated. However, if a room sits idle, patients *can* still be treated. An ED bed might be a bottleneck, but it should not be the resource that directs flow. It is therefore not the constraint.

Nursing should not be the constraint, either. Nurses' scope of practice is more limited than physicians, and their activities are typically coordinated around physician activities, not the other way around. Physicians generate care tasks that nurses then execute, rather than the converse. Nursing workflow is largely dictated by the pace of the physician. Although ED nurses work their butts off, their activities should not determine flow in the department. Nursing is therefore not the constraint.

If the physician is the constraint, then ideally there should be only one scenario in which the physician is idle—when there are no more patients to see. In this scenario, the constraint is no longer the physician; it is now the marketplace. If the physician is idle in any other situation, it is because a nonconstraint resource has become a bottleneck (e.g., no rooms, gurneys, or chairs available for the next patient, not enough nursing resources to accommodate additional patients). To identify times when the physician might be idle, we need to move to the second focusing step.

Step 2: Decide How to Exploit the Constraint

In Step 1, we identified the ED physician as the system's constraint. To exploit the constraint in step 2, we must find where in the workflow the physician sits idle.

The constraint is idle when there are new patients to see but the physician is not actively engaged in patient care; patient encounters take too long because the physician is engaged in nonvalue tasks; or the physician performs nonconstraint-level tasks.

To protect the constraint from being idle, we need to employ the tools we learned in the previous chapter, namely, VSM, full kit, DBR, and Buffer Management.

First, we will utilize VSM to identify the time the physician spends on non-value activities (we will identify the nonvalue activities here in the second focusing step and then work to shorten or eliminate them in the third focusing step). Our VSM exercise can be even less detailed than exhibit 8.3. We simply need to make a list of the activities in the physician's workflow and then see which ones add value from the perspective of the patient. We start VSM by mapping out a typical constraint workflow.

Exhibit 9.1 outlines an ED physician's activities during a patient encounter. We could add detail to this map by estimating the average duration of each activity, but for our purposes, a simple list of the activities will suffice.

Next, we designate the activities as either adding value or not adding value from the patient's perspective. As such, the activities that add value are those that directly move the patient toward a disposition (i.e., admission or discharge) and treat the patient's condition. From a practical standpoint, there are activities in exhibit 9.1 that the physician will need to complete; from a VSM standpoint, however, these steps do not add value from the patient's point of view.

Activities that add value include:

- Review chart
- Take a history
- Examine patient
- Write orders
- Look up results
- Recheck patient
- Call primary care physician or consulting physicians (if the call immediately impacts patient care)
- Admit or discharge patient

Activities that do not add value include:

- Sign up
- Walk to room
- Start charting

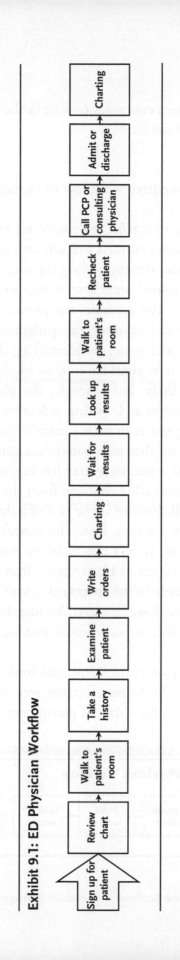

Exhibit 9.1: ED Physician Workflow

Sign up for patient → Review chart → Walk to patient's room → Take a history → Examine patient → Write orders → Charting → Wait for results → Look up results → Walk to patient's room → Recheck patient → Call PCP or consulting physician → Admit or discharge → Charting

- Wait for results
- Walk back to room
- All the time the patient continues to wait in the ED after the admit or discharge order has been written
- Complete charting

We can revise the ED physician workflow to include only the activities that add value (exhibit 9.2).

VSM has enabled us to exploit the constraint by removing activities that do not add value to the patient's visit. As a result, each patient encounter requires less of the ED physician's time, thereby adding capacity to the constraint.

The caveat to this revised workflow is that some of the activities we have removed are unavoidable. For example, the physician must walk to the patient's room to take a history and examine the patient, even though walking to the patient's room does not add value. By identifying the activities that do not add value, however, we can now consider how to minimize those activities that we cannot eliminate completely. For example, the physician could minimize the time spent walking to rooms and writing orders by bringing a mobile computer workstation and writing orders in each patient's room rather than returning to a separate desk or workspace after each patient encounter.

Likewise, charting is a necessary activity, but it doesn't add value from the patient's perspective. Eliminating charting from the workflow would require the physician to complete all charting at the end of a shift. While this would remove a large amount of nonvalue time from the workflow, it would also negatively impact physician wellness. It isn't reasonable to expect anyone to finish a busy shift only to then face a stack of blank charts from all of the patients seen that day. We acknowledged early in the chapter that staff wellness cannot be sacrificed in the name of improved flow. However, by identifying charting as such a large nonvalue step in the VSM, we now know that we must address it in the next focusing step.

Finally, we need to protect the constraint from having either too few or too many new patients to see. In the next focusing step, we can employ DBR to schedule the release of new material—that is, placing new patients where the physician

Exhibit 9.2: Revised ED Physician Workflow

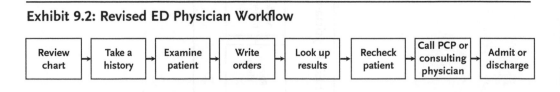

can evaluate them—and Buffer Management to protect the constraint from the inevitable variations and delays that occur in the ED.

Step 3: Subordinate Everything Else to the Constraint

In the second focusing step, we made the decision to exploit the constraint. In the ED, we have decided that the ED physician should never sit idle when there is a new patient to see. The time spent on each patient encounter should be shortened by minimizing activities that do not add value from the patient's perspective. The constraint should perform only constraint-level tasks. Before the constraint even sees a new patient, all of the supplies and information needed to treat the patient and make a disposition should be readily available. There should always be a new patient ready and waiting for the constraint, but the constraint should not be overwhelmed by having too many new patients ready at the same time. Now we have to figure out how to make it all happen.

DBR

Let's start by applying DBR to ED flow. As the constraint, the ED physician is the drum; the speed at which the physician sees new patients sets the pace of the department. All the activities in the ED must be synchronized to the pace of the physician. How quickly the physician can see new patients dictates the rate at which we should bring patients from the waiting room into the ED (whether in a room, on a gurney in a hallway, or on a chair) for evaluation.

In this model, the buffer is a patient buffer. The buffer protects the drum from running out of material and sitting idle, so in our example, the ED physician should always have a buffer of new patients ready for evaluation. The size of the buffer is determined by the productivity of the provider. A slower provider might require a buffer of two patients, whereas a faster or more efficient provider might require four patients as a buffer. As soon as the provider finishes up with one patient, the buffer should ensure that there is always another patient ready for evaluation. When the physician signs up to see the next patient, the buffer needs to be replenished—that is, another patient needs to be brought back from the waiting room.

The rope ties the release of new patients (e.g., bringing them back to a room or placing them on a gurney) to the physician's pace. The rope is a signal that can be triggered once the patient buffer is consumed. A specific staff member in the ED must be responsible for first recognizing that the physician has signed up to see another patient, thereby consuming some of the buffer, and then replenishing the buffer with a new patient. The rope mechanism should ideally be managed by a flow nurse whose sole job is to manage flow in the department; in most EDs, however, the rope is probably managed by a charge nurse. The construct of charge nurse as rope is problematic, as the activities of the rope must be subordinate to the drum. An ED charge nurse has many responsibilities that are not related to flow (staff management, ambulance arrivals, and phone calls, to name just a few). As a result, it is often difficult for a charge nurse to stay focused on bringing new patients back from the waiting room (replenishing the buffer) at the pace of the drum.

Keep in mind that the buffer protects the constraint from inevitable variations, delays, or glitches in the system. In the ED, the likelihood of delays in the system is closely related to the rope. The more distracted the person in charge of the rope is, the more likely it becomes that the buffer will be consumed without replenishment.

Imagine an ED with a single physician, ten patients in the waiting room, five ED patient rooms, and an ideal buffer of three patients.[1] When the physician signs up for a new patient, there are two patients remaining in the buffer. The buffer is now in the yellow (one-third has been consumed), which triggers a signal (the rope) to the charge nurse to bring another patient back from the waiting room. There are now nine patients in the waiting room and four patients in ED rooms, three of whom haven't been seen by the physician. The ED will have good flow if it can continue in this manner. If the charge nurse has to deal with an extraneous problem, however, a new patient may not get placed in a room to replenish the buffer. If the physician then moves on to evaluate the next patient, two-thirds of the buffer will be consumed and the buffer will be in the red. If the physician picks up the final patient who is ready to be seen, the buffer will have been totally consumed (the buffer is now in the black). If the buffer is not replenished, the physician will sit idle, even though there are still patients in the waiting room who have yet to be seen.

We can draw a number of conclusions from this hypothetical scenario. If the person in charge of the rope will inevitably be distracted by activities other than supporting flow (buffer replenishment), then the buffer should probably be bigger than what the constraint requires. A larger buffer is not ideal, however, because one of the purposes of DBR is to avoid releasing too much inventory into the system. A better solution would be to have a person who can be dedicated to managing the rope (a dedicated flow nurse, for example) without a lot of other tasks competing for his or her attention. Alternatively, we can build a redundancy for buffer replenishment into the system. If the buffer moves into the yellow third, other nurses in the ED, such as triage nurses and float nurses, could recognize that as a signal to make a backup plan—for example, if the charge nurse still isn't available to replenish the buffer, then the triage nurse will immediately bring two new patients back from the waiting room. Then, if the buffer turns red (the physician has signed up to see the last patient in the buffer), the triage nurse will execute the plan and refill the buffer.

If it isn't yet clear, the system we are describing challenges the orthodoxy of ED flow. Thought leaders in ED flow might consider it blasphemous to recommend keeping patients in the waiting room if the ED has empty beds. The concept of "pull till full," which dictates doing everything possible to move patients out of the waiting room and into an ED bed, has been a tenet of ED management for years. The rationale behind "pull till full" is manifold: It is assumed that patients receive better care if they wait in an ED bed instead of the waiting room; evaluation and treatment can begin sooner if the patient is already in an ED bed; reducing door-to-room time also reduces door-to-provider time; and patient satisfaction is higher when door-to-room times are shorter. These assumptions may be valid in an ED that doesn't properly staff its triage or struggles to bring patients back even when there are available ED beds, but "pull till full" acts as a workaround instead of addressing core issues.

There are downsides to releasing too much raw material or too many parts into a system such as a factory; so, too, are there downsides to having too many patients ready for the physician. "Pull till full" loads up patient rooms without concern for the provider workload; it does not synchronize new patient release to the pace of the drum. When there is a high volume of patients in ED rooms, waiting for the physician, the physician succumbs to multitasking. Multitasking is one of the biggest enemies of efficient flow—regardless of how good we think we are at it (Westbrook et al. 2018). Furthermore, physicians will be interrupted with questions about patients who are in the ED much more frequently than they would be interrupted if those same patients were left in the waiting room. This is true even if the physician has not yet signed up for the patient. Each interruption creates a delay in flow and compounds the inefficiencies of multitasking.

Another risk is leapfrogging, also known as expediting. In leapfrogging or expediting, a physician will be pulled off course from seeing the next patient in line because a nurse is advocating for a different patient to be seen instead. Most likely, that nurse knows only about his or her own few patients, not all the patients in the department. The different patient may be that nurse's sickest patient, but is not necessarily the sickest patient in the entire department, or even sicker than the next patient in line. When the physician is pulled into a room unexpectedly, especially to see a stable patient, it upsets the rhythm of the constraint and adds to the delay in flow.

"Pull till full" also increases the likelihood that the ED physician will start a task without a full kit. When multiple patients are placed in rooms in batches or in quick succession, the next patient may not yet be in a gown; the physician may be in a rush and overlook an important triage note; or the provider may see the patient before the patient receives an electrocardiogram (EKG) and forget to go back and review the results when the test has been completed.

Finally, from the perspective of VSM, any time that the patient spends waiting is time that does not add value, regardless of where the waiting occurs. It is no more valuable to the patient, then, to wait in an ED room as opposed to the waiting room. Proponents of "pull till full" argue otherwise; the time it takes to place a patient into an ED room is assumed to be an important determinant of patient satisfaction. Patient satisfaction, however, is a fuzzy science at best, and this assumption is not an absolute.[2]

We have identified a cogent rationale for controlling the release of new patients from the waiting room to the ED as well as the downsides of "pull till full." However, we are responsible for all the patients in the ED, regardless of their location, and keeping patients in the waiting room could make the ratio of waiting room patients to triage nurses too high, especially relative to the ratio of ED patients to bedside nurses. As we acknowledged earlier, patient safety cannot be compromised in the name of flow. If there are not enough triage nurses to keep up with the volume of waiting room patients, then one or more bedside nurses should be reassigned to triage. There will likely be bedside nurses available for reassignment since we are now controlling the volume of patients being moved to ED beds. Likewise, if regulating the release of new patients causes the ED waiting room to fill up, we should have extra nursing capacity in the ED that can shift to triage, at least temporarily.

One final comment about "pull till full": If the resource in charge of the rope (i.e., the charge nurse) is always too distracted to consistently replenish the buffer, then "pull till full" may be an appropriate fallback approach. It is better to have too many patients waiting for the provider than to have the physician sit idle because there are not enough patients who are ready to be seen. Multitasking and interruptions are problematic but not as bad as having the constraint sit idle. "Pull till full" can act as a proxy for the rope, but the goal should be to make the rope work effectively![3]

Full Kitting

In traditional workflow, the physician sees a new patient, takes a history and examines the patient, orders tests, and, eventually, reviews the test results, returns to the patient, and makes a decision regarding admission or discharge. This workflow requires multiple touch points for the constraint; in an ideal workflow, all the required tests would already be ordered, performed, and resulted by the time the physician sees a patient. The constraint would then have only one touch point: The physician would be able to take a history, examine the new patient, review the test results, and decide whether to admit or discharge the patient immediately. Streamlining the physician's process is an example of full kitting. Everything the physician needs to complete the task (in this case, evaluating, treating, and making a disposition) is ready when the physician begins the task.

A byproduct of controlling the release of new patients into the ED area is that patients spend more time in triage or in the waiting room, where we can apply nurse-initiated order sets, or NIOS. NIOS are lists of standing orders that are applied based on a patient's chief complaint and tailored to information obtained during triage. The idea behind NIOS is that most patients with certain presenting symptoms will need roughly the same set of labs and imaging studies. For example, most patients over 40 who come to the ED with chest pain will need a complete blood count, a chemistry panel, a troponin, an EKG, and a chest x-ray. When a patient presents to triage with chest pain, this order set is triggered: Blood is drawn and sent to the lab, the x-ray is ordered, and an EKG is obtained. When the patient is brought into the ED to fill the buffer, all the test results are ready and waiting for the physician. In the new, more efficient workflow, the physician picks up a new patient, obtains a history, examines the patient, reviews the completed test results, either admits or discharges the patient, and then moves on to the next patient. This is full kitting at its best! In this scenario, the physician needs to interact with the patient only one time instead of repeatedly. Even if a second touch point is required (a repeat troponin, perhaps, or a recheck after receiving medication), NIOS reduce the number of touch points and thereby improve the constraint's productivity.

As you can imagine, this works only if NIOS err on the side of inclusivity. If a blood count and chemistry panel are ordered, but the patient also needs a troponin, then having the blood count and chemistry results doesn't necessarily help with flow. For this reason, NIOS should be overly inclusive rather than too limited. The downside of such an approach is that some tests may end up being unnecessary in hindsight; however, the improvement in flow outweighs the potential downside.

Since ED providers are ultimately responsible for all orders, the ED physician group must develop the NIOS; order sets should be evidence-based and reflect best practices. As an additional benefit, standardizing order sets will reduce variability among providers (one of the aims of Six Sigma). It makes sense that physicians should be evaluating any given patient with chest pain the same way and with the same tests as their colleagues. Of course, nothing precludes a provider from ordering additional tests after evaluating a patient, but if the NIOS are effective, then additional orders should be the exception and not the rule.

Full kitting can also protect the constraint from performing tasks that can be done by nonconstraints. To do so, we must create a list of all the activities that physicians find themselves doing that could be done by someone else. For example, physicians often spend time looking for missing equipment or supplies used in common procedures. Another staff member could be responsible for stocking the equipment used for procedures such as suturing, draining abscesses, intubating patients, placing central lines, and performing point of care ultrasounds. Moreover, the person responsible for stocking equipment could also be responsible for placing the equipment in close proximity to where it is typically needed. We identify the opportunities for full kitting in the second focusing step; in the third focusing step, we can assign responsibility for full kitting and create a signal for replenishment.

Buffer Management

We have already discussed how to use buffer consumption to prioritize and expedite activities so that the constraint never sits idle. If we have a buffer of three patients, then the number of patients "consumed" signals how urgently we need to add patients to the buffer. The buffer also coordinates the activities of other employees so that the buffer is replenished even when the rope (usually the charge nurse) is busy.

Buffer Management also allows us to quickly pinpoint when and where a problem has arisen that may impact flow. If the charge nurse notices that the buffer is frequently in the red or black, there is likely a problem upstream of the constraint. Perhaps there is a delay in the triage process, and another nurse needs to move to triage. Triage could be so overwhelmed that the triage nurse is too busy to bring new patients into ED rooms; in this case, a tech could be dispatched to get the patients.

Likewise, if the charge nurse notices that the buffer is not being consumed (it remains green or yellow for long periods of time), there may be a delay at the constraint. Perhaps the provider is caring for an unstable patient who requires a lot of attention or is stuck in a procedure that is taking longer than expected.

In some instances, the buffer may grow larger (e.g., there are already three patients in the buffer, then a sick patient comes through triage and needs to be roomed immediately, then an ambulance brings in an injured patient who also needs a bed). The provider may be overwhelmed by multiple critical patients who are too unstable to remain in the waiting room. In these cases, the patient buffer may signal to the charge nurse that the ED should consider going on ambulance diversion until the physician can catch up. Tracking buffer consumption alerts us when there is an unexpected problem and helps focus our troubleshooting.

Keep in mind that a patient doesn't have to wait until NIOS have been performed and test results have been returned before being brought to a room. If the patient buffer needs replenishing and the next patient hasn't completed NIOS, it is better to bring the patient back to a room and fill the buffer.

A Quick Return to VSM

Now that we have designed ED operations around the DBR construct, employed full kit, and utilized Buffer Management for prioritizing and expediting, let's return to VSM. In exhibit 9.2, we shortened or eliminated many activities in the constraint's workflow that did not add value to the patient. We have subsequently used our other tools to further refine the workflow. At this point in subordination, it is worth revisiting exhibit 9.2 to see if there are any final, obvious refinements left to make.

Putting It All Together

We have now applied all of our new tools—VSM, DBR, Buffer Management, and full kitting—to ED flow. A new diagram of idealized ED flow appears in exhibit 9.3.

In exhibit 9.3, a patient checks in to be seen and is brought back to triage, where NIOS are applied. Tests are ordered and blood is drawn; the patient then returns to the waiting room while the tests are running. Meanwhile, the physician evaluates new patients from the patient buffer, one at a time. As the physician sees a new patient, the rope signals the appropriate resource (e.g., the charge nurse) to move another patient from the waiting room into an ED room to replenish the patient buffer. The rate at which the charge nurse "releases" a new patient from the waiting room is controlled by the pace at which the physician sees new patients in the buffer. If the patient has been in the waiting room area long enough, then the test results will be ready by the time the physician goes in to evaluate the patient (full kit). After evaluating a new patient, the physician checks for any possible dispositions among the patients who have already been seen. If there is a disposition, that patient is admitted or discharged, and the physician then checks for another possible disposition. This process continues until there are no more patients ready to admit or discharge, at which point the physician picks up a new patient from the patient buffer. The physician's activities are streamlined to minimize the nonvalue activities identified in VSM (while keeping provider wellness in mind). In TOC terms, the drum sets the pace, the rope chokes the release of new materials at the point of the waiting room, and the buffer protects the constraint from running out of new materials in the event of a delay in the upstream processes.

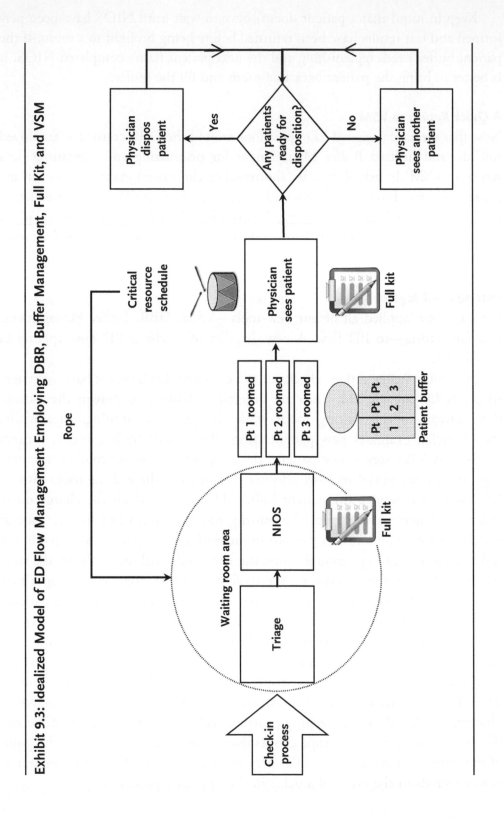

Exhibit 9.3: Idealized Model of ED Flow Management Employing DBR, Buffer Management, Full Kit, and VSM

STEP 4: ELEVATE THE CONSTRAINT

After subordinating all other activities to support the constraint, there may still be inadequate provider capacity to manage patient volumes in the ED. At this point, we must consider investing in additional capacity for the constraint. Since the physician is the constraint, and since the physician is both the costliest resource and the most difficult resource to replace, we must be strategic about adding constraint capacity.

The most obvious option for increasing constraint capacity is to add another physician. Before doing so, however, we should consider opportunities for augmenting the productivity of the physicians who are already working in the ED. For example, we could use scribes for nonconstraint tasks, such as charting or looking up test results, that physicians traditionally perform. While scribes cannot perform constraint-level activities (e.g., evaluating and treating patients), they can reduce many of the activities that do not add value. If a physician does not have to spend part of a shift on charting, then there will be more time to see new patients. Utilizing scribes can be a cost-effective way to both minimize nonvalue activities (e.g., charting) and promote provider wellness (avoiding that stack of blank charts at the end of the day).

Another opportunity for increasing productivity is to pay off-duty ED physicians for on-call shifts in case there is a surge in patient volume. The on-call physician(s) could come into the ED and start working once patient volume reaches a predetermined threshold. Paying physicians to be on call is an investment that adds capacity to the constraint but costs less than creating an additional full-time, or even part-time, position. Investing in extra constraint capacity that ultimately may not be needed creates another kind of buffer—a resource buffer or a "bench." The resource buffer is analogous to a basketball team: There is both a starting lineup and a bench of subs, who may or may not play, depending on how the starting lineup performs.

We can also consider using less expensive providers, such as physician assistants and nurse practitioners (known collectively as advanced practice providers, or APPs), to improve productivity. While APPs may not have the same scope as physicians, the cost per unit of care delivered is considerably lower with an APP as compared to a physician: Two hours of APP coverage typically costs less than one hour of physician coverage. APPs are especially helpful for managing a relatively large volume of lower-acuity patients.

We have now maximized the productivity of our current constraint resource. There is an on-call system in place, and we have hired scribes and APPs. If the ED still can't keep up with patient volume, we will now have to hire another ED physician. Before we make this costly investment, however, we must first ensure that all the other resources in the system are capable of managing the increase in volume that will come with the increase in constraint capacity.

In effective constraint management, all nonconstraint resources must have sufficient excess or protective capacity to handle the increase in volume that results from adding constraint capacity. It would be foolish to invest in the most expensive resource (a new physician), only to have that resource sit idle because there aren't enough nurses, housekeepers, laboratory technicians, or respiratory therapists to accommodate a greater volume of patients. If the constraint sits idle because nonconstraint resources lack adequate capacity, then we have turned a nonconstraint into a bottleneck. We must, therefore, analyze the available capacity of the nonconstraint resources—and increase their capacity, if needed—*before* hiring another physician.

Once we decide to hire an additional ED physician, we must be strategic about when to add the extra constraint capacity—in terms of time of day, days of the week, and time of year.

Patients present to the ED in a predictable pattern, regardless of ED location, size, or time of year. Exhibit 9.4 shows the typical volume of patients that presents to the ED each hour of the day. The shape of the curve is ubiquitous: Patients arrive to every ED in roughly the same pattern. The amplitude of the curve (i.e., the volume of patients) in exhibit 9.4 may increase or decrease—depending on the day of the week, the time of year, or the size of the department—but the overall shape of the curve remains the same. By examining exhibit 9.4, we can tailor additional physician hours (additional constraint capacity) to the peak volumes of the curve, such as between 10:00 a.m. and 10:00 p.m.

Exhibit 9.4: Volume Curve of ED Patient Arrival Throughout the Day

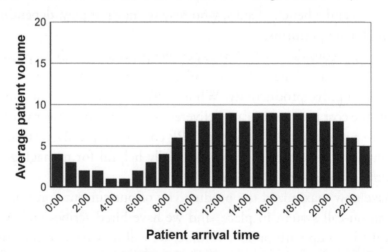

STEP 5: DO NOT LET INERTIA BECOME THE NEW SYSTEM CONSTRAINT

After completing the first four focusing steps, it is time to step back, observe the revised ED flow, and identify areas where problems keep occurring—in other words, continuous process improvement. If workflow seems easy and employees rarely have to put out fires, then we should see if there are times when the ED physician sits idle, and specifically because no new patients are waiting to be seen. If so, then the constraint is no longer the ED physician; it is the marketplace. The implication is that the ED now has excess capacity and can work to increase patient volume—an exciting position to be in. While growing the business, we can continue to apply VSM to the constraint process and fine-tune operations through additional iterations of our DBR and Buffer Management tools.

On the other hand, if the ED physician is sitting idle while there are still patients waiting to be seen, then we need to find out why. In the context of Buffer Management, the patient buffer might be consistently two-thirds or fully consumed (red or black), or the buffer might rarely need replenishing (i.e., the buffer is consumed too slowly). If the buffer is chronically too full or too empty, it signals a need for project improvement to determine what process in the system is responsible for the deficiency.

If physician coverage continues to seem inadequate, especially when certain providers are working, it might be valuable to examine variations in physician practices. Do all ED physicians have similar admission rates? Do they utilize tests with the same frequency? Are lengths of stay for admitted and discharged patients similar among providers? If outliers in physician practices can be identified (especially for providers who have higher admission rates, utilize more tests, and have longer patient lengths of stay), educational intervention or best-practice guidelines may reduce variability.

Another possibility is that a nonconstraint has become a new bottleneck. It is imperative to recognize when a new bottleneck is impeding constraint productivity. For example, if the ED physician is sitting idle because the ED is running out of rooms to place patients in, then we should subordinate to the new bottleneck and change where the provider can see new patients. Lower-acuity patients could be examined in a gurney and then moved to a chair (or even back to the waiting room) instead of being placed in a bed. A provider could move to triage and quickly evaluate and discharge low-acuity patients. If there are nursing shortages, we could revise sick leave policies or create a resource pool to cover holes in the schedule. We may need to temporarily play defense again, using the skills from part I of this book to identify and break bottlenecks. Then after the bottlenecks have been broken, we can return to playing offense, using the principles of constraint management as the playbook.

SUMMARY

- Improving flow in the ED increases throughput in the hospital system.
- In the ED, the ED physician is the constraint.
- VSM helps eliminate activities in the physician's workflow that do not add value.
- Full kitting helps prepare patients for the physician and minimizes the wait time and number of touch points for the constraint that is associated with each patient encounter.
- To exploit the constraint, we must protect the physician from running out of patients to see, performing nonphysician tasks, multitasking, leapfrogging, and interruptions.
- The physician is the drum in DBR, and new patients are roomed in the ED based on the pace of the physician.
- There should always be a patient buffer that is large enough (but not too large) to protect the physician from becoming idle.
- The rope is managed by a staff member, ideally a flow nurse but often the charge nurse, who makes sure that the buffer is replenished by rooming new patients at the pace of the physician.
- We can track patient buffer consumption to identify and quickly troubleshoot developing flow problems.
- NIOS help facilitate full kitting by gathering all the information the physician might need to treat, admit, or discharge a patient while the patient is still in the waiting room.

NOTES

1. When we have more than one provider, we adjust the buffer accordingly. If we have a buffer of three patients when one provider is working, for example, we can increase buffer size to five or six patients when two providers are working.

2. If you are interested in patient satisfaction, David Maister's "The Psychology of Waiting Lines" is an amazing read (Maister 1985). Maister asserts that occupied time feels shorter than unoccupied time. Uncertain waits feel longer than known waits; unexplained waits feel longer than explained waits; unfair waits feel longer than equitable waits; solo waits feel longer than group waits; and the more valuable the service, the longer the customer will wait. Based on Maister's observations, it does not necessarily hold that patient satisfaction improves with shorter door-to-bed times, as reducing such times does not address uncertain or unexpected waits. In fact, moving a patient from the waiting room to an ED room could turn a group wait into a solo wait, which could decrease satisfaction. Additionally, if the time a patient spends in the waiting room is used productively, the wait feels like

occupied time in which the patient is receiving valuable service. Waiting room time, as well as time spent in triage, can be productive through the use of nurse-initiated order sets (NIOS), in which the nurse orders tests, draws blood, or obtains imaging. The results can be ready by the time the physician sees the patient, which not only helps with flow but also improves the patient's perception of wait time.

3. "Pull till full" is also a viable strategy when the ED bed is a bottleneck; in such a case, we do not need to limit the rate at which we move patients from the waiting room. By definition, the ED bed as bottleneck limits flow and is hampering the constraint's productivity, and if a bed is not filled as soon as it becomes available, then we are not exploiting the bottleneck.

REFERENCES

Maister, D. H. 1985. "The Psychology of Waiting Lines." In *The Service Encounter: Managing Employee/Customer Interaction in Service Businesses*, edited by J. A. Czepiel, M. R. Solomon, and C. F. Surprenant, 113–24. Lexington, MA: Lexington Books.

Westbrook, J. I., M. Z. Raban, S. R. Walter, and H. Douglas. 2018. "Task Errors by Emergency Physicians Are Associated with Interruptions, Multitasking, Fatigue and Working Memory Capacity: A Prospective, Direct Observation Study." *BMJ Quality & Safety* 27 (8): 655–63.

CHAPTER 10

Using Buffer Management to Facilitate Inpatient Unit Flow

OBJECTIVES

- Apply the 5FS to constraint management on an inpatient unit
- Identify the constraint on an inpatient unit
- Use Buffer Management to improve patient flow and reduce lengths of stay

---

IN A HOSPITAL SYSTEM, teamwork is vital to patient care, staff well-being, and patient flow. Teamwork is especially important on inpatient units; patients with many different conditions may reside on the same unit, and staff must coordinate not only with each other but also with teams on other units. Every employee has a personal agenda and is held accountable for a unique set of responsibilities. Coordinating these resources is one of the greatest challenges to improving inpatient flow, and the solution largely depends on teamwork and cooperation.

The huddle is a key concept in resource coordination, and it serves as the backbone of constraint management for inpatient flow. Huddles are standing meetings, usually 5–15 minutes long, that occur every morning or at the beginning of each shift. Their purpose is to create action items to deal with the immediate issues of the day. It is assumed that unexpected events will arise, so it is preferable to discuss contingencies at the beginning of the day or shift. To be effective, daily huddles must be multidisciplinary, allowing for different perspectives on impending issues (Stewart and Johnson 2007). Agenda items can include

- reviewing the daily patient list to make sure full kits are in place;
- determining if any patients have unique needs that may require extra time or additional resources;
- confirming staff and provider schedules to determine availability throughout the day and to help coordinate resources among patients, specialties, and units; and
- checking the status of the buffers to set priorities and record data that may be useful for continuous improvement projects.

Huddles can quickly resolve quality and flow problems, improve patient care, improve communication among all the stakeholders, and foster a sense of teamwork and community. We will dive deeper into the huddle concept later in the chapter.

STEP 1: IDENTIFY THE CONSTRAINT

As we did in our assessment of the ED, management of inpatient flow starts with identifying the constraint. Inpatient care usually requires many different types of staff resources, so it is hard to label a single position or provider as the dominant resource. For some patients, the physician may have the most direct impact on patient care, but in other instances, the physical therapist, social worker, or nurse may be the most resource-intensive part of a patient's hospital course.

In every case, a number of different resources must be synchronized in order for a patient to be discharged. Discharge, then, is a focal point of coordination—but the discharge itself isn't a resource, so it doesn't qualify as a constraint. From a flow standpoint, however, the patient's discharge represents, and is represented by, the availability of an inpatient bed. We can therefore consider the inpatient bed to be the constraint. All the activities on an inpatient unit must be coordinated to support the patient's discharge, which subsequently creates an available patient bed. (Note that discharge is a proxy for a patient's condition improving, indicating that the patient no longer needs to remain in the hospital. Coordinating resources to support a discharge, therefore, is analogous to coordinating resources to support a patient's getting better, which is the ultimate goal of patient care.) Conveniently, we have already spent significant time considering the inpatient bed as a bottleneck, and much of the strategy we discussed to manage the inpatient bed as a bottleneck is applicable to the inpatient bed as the constraint.

STEP 2: EXPLOIT THE CONSTRAINT

We have defined an available inpatient bed as one that is clean, staffed, and ready to accept a new patient. As a constraint, the "productivity" of the inpatient bed—

how efficiently patients are treated and discharged—dictates the productivity of the unit. The inpatient bed should not sit idle, nor should it perform nonconstraint tasks.

To prevent the constraint from sitting idle, there should never be a clean, staffed bed sitting empty if a patient somewhere in the hospital needs that bed. The patient in need could be a postoperative patient from the recovery unit, an ICU patient ready to step down to a floor bed, or an ED patient who needs to be admitted. Often, inpatient beds are held open and empty while waiting for elective-surgery patients or while an inpatient unit spends excessive time reviewing an ED patient's chart to see if the patient is "appropriate" for the unit. These examples are only a couple of obvious activities that do not add value and should be reduced or eliminated.

We can also exploit the inpatient bed by minimizing the time it spends on nonconstraint tasks. In this case, an inpatient bed is performing a nonconstraint task anytime it is occupied by a patient who no longer needs it. This includes times when

- the patient is ready for discharge, but the physician has not yet written the order;
- the discharge order has been written, but the patient's nurse has not yet discharged the patient (or not yet flagged the room as empty in the hospital's electronic bed inventory system);
- the discharge order has been written, but the patient is waiting for a ride home, a prescription, discharge teaching, or durable medical equipment; or
- the patient no longer needs acute care and is ready for discharge, but there is no appropriate place for the patient to go (e.g., a skilled nursing facility, an assisted living facility, adult foster care).

Finally, we can exploit the constraint by finding ways to shorten patient lengths of stay. We will tackle execution of these strategies in our discussion of the third focusing step.

STEP 3: SUBORDINATE EVERYTHING ELSE TO THE CONSTRAINT

A clean, staffed bed often sits empty for hours, even though there is a patient somewhere in the hospital who needs that bed. Other times, a bed may be empty but not available to accept a patient, possibly because there is no nurse to staff the bed, because the bed is dirty and housekeeping doesn't know it needs to be cleaned, or because bed control doesn't know that the bed has already been cleaned. Alternately, the patient in that bed may have been discharged but is waiting for a ride home. The patient may have even left the room, but the room hasn't been flagged as available in the hospital's bed inventory system.

We have discussed how to subordinate workflow to improve capacity when the inpatient bed is the bottleneck. You may benefit from reviewing chapters 1–6 and reframing the strategies discussed for inpatient beds as the constraint resource rather than the bottleneck. Instead of rehashing those concepts, let's focus on a new strategy: shortening the average inpatient length of stay (i.e., from when a patient is admitted to when the patient is ready for discharge). Shortening lengths of stay requires multiple resources—social workers, nurses, physical therapists, physicians, pharmacists, and others—to work toward a common goal. We can use Buffer Management to coordinate all of these resources and protect the constraint.

When a patient is admitted to the hospital, the admitting physician typically estimates how long the patient will need to stay before being ready for discharge—in many hospitals, such estimates are documented at the time of admission. Physician estimates are usually fairly accurate, both for unplanned admissions from the ED (e.g., pneumonia, ischemic heart disease, trauma) and for patients undergoing scheduled procedures. Anticipated discharge times are based on a physician's personal experience, cohort comparisons (i.e., the average length of stay at the hospital or within a practice group), and independent benchmarks. There are also a number of published benchmarks for expected lengths of stay that are adjusted for patient acuity. More recently, predictive analytics have been employed to refine anticipated discharge times. Having a fairly accurate estimate for a patient's length of stay allows us to do two things:

1. As the expected discharge date approaches, everyone involved in the patient's care knows if the patient is on track to discharge on time or if resources need to be redirected (or expedited) to get the patient back on track.
2. When discharges are delayed (for reasons other than unexpected complications or the patient not responding to treatment), the reasons for the delay can be tracked; tracking the reasons for delays informs ongoing process improvement efforts.

Buffer Management on an Inpatient Unit

When a patient is admitted to the hospital, we consider the anticipated length of stay as the buffer—specifically, a time buffer. Depending on the length of stay, the buffer is measured in hours or days. As the patient's hospital course progresses, the buffer gets consumed. If the anticipated discharge date approaches, and it seems as though the patient's discharge may be delayed, then resources can be synchronized, prioritized, and possibly expedited to meet the patient's discharge time. Comparing buffer consumption among patients helps staff coordinate and prioritize their daily activities, with patients whose buffers have the greatest consumption receiving top priority.

Let's consider a couple of examples.

Example 1

A 54-year-old woman is admitted to the hospital after elective orthopedic surgery. Her anticipated length of stay is three days. The resources involved in the patient's care include a surgeon, nurses, physical therapists, and pharmacists. The buffer for her admission is three days. In her first day at the hospital, less than one-third of the buffer has been consumed (green). In her second day at the hospital, between one-third and two-thirds of the buffer has been consumed (yellow). In her third day at the hospital, more than two-thirds of the buffer has been consumed (red). If the patient is still in the hospital on day four, all of the buffer has been consumed (black).

The patient's care team meets briefly every morning to track the patient's progress and ensure the patient's anticipated discharge date will not be delayed. The color code helps the care team coordinate how much time is left to complete their respective tasks for the patient. If one of the resources is not on target, the color code tells the team how to prioritize this patient. If, for example, the buffer is in the yellow and physical therapy services are running behind schedule, the team should create a plan for physical therapy to catch up (e.g., add an extra session, re-prioritize this patient over another physical therapy patient whose buffer is in the green). The team doesn't have to act on the plan if the buffer is yellow, simply create a plan (just in case). However, if the buffer turns red and physical therapy is still running behind, then the team must execute its plan. Moreover, the team must prioritize getting this patient physical therapy over providing services to patients whose buffers are in the green and yellow.

Another advantage of using Buffer Management is that if the patient is expected to leave the hospital in three days and the pharmacist has to facilitate a few hours of medication teaching, the pharmacist can be flexible about meeting with this patient. The pharmacist can plan out his or her schedule, prioritize other patients whose needs are more immediate, and coordinate medication-related resources across the system more effectively.

Example 2

A 78-year-old man presents to the ED with sepsis. The patient is intubated and admitted to the ICU. His anticipated length of stay is 12 days. During days 1–4 of his hospital stay, less than one-third of the buffer has been consumed (green).

During days 5–8, between one-third and two-thirds of the buffer has been consumed (yellow). During days 6–9, between two-thirds and 100 percent of the buffer has been consumed (red). If the patient is still in the hospital on day 13, all of the buffer will have been consumed (black).

This patient will have a larger care team and require more resources than the patient in the first example, because he is both older and sicker than the middle-aged woman having elective surgery. The patient's care will span at least two units (the ICU and an inpatient unit), and he will most likely be discharged to a skilled nursing facility. More complicated and potentially more unpredictable cases require an even higher level of resource coordination as well as vigilance to ensure that the patient is discharged on time.

Suppose our patient has been in the hospital for nine days. The buffer is in the red, but the patient is out of the ICU and doing well—he is on track to be discharged by day 12. Then the patient aspirates and ends up back in the ICU. His anticipated length of stay is revised upward, from 12 days to 16 days. The measurement of buffer consumption should be adjusted accordingly. Nine days have still been consumed, but with a bigger buffer, total consumption is now at 56 percent (9 days out of 16) instead of 75 percent (9 days out of 12). The buffer has moved back into the yellow. The buffer may be adjusted if the patient's anticipated length of stay needs to be increased for medical reasons, as in this example of aspiration. However, if the length of stay increases due to *nonmedical* reasons (e.g., the surgeon discharged the patient too late in the day; physical therapy was late one day and couldn't spend enough time with the patient; the patient missed physical therapy because he was getting an imaging scan; the social worker thought the patient would go home, but the patient's family now says they are unable to care for him) then the time buffer is *not* adjusted. We cannot always predict changes in a patient's condition or an unexpected response to treatment, but we should be able to control the nonmedical factors—the factors largely responsible for poor patient flow.

Comparing the lengths of stay in the two preceding examples illustrates an important point: If a patient is supposed to be in the hospital for one day but stays two days, it seems like a huge delay in discharge. The patient's length of stay is 100 percent longer than expected. If, however, a patient's anticipated length of stay is 20 days and the actual length of stay is 21 days, it doesn't seem like a big deal; the percentage delay is much lower. Often, the longer the anticipated length of stay, the less urgency there is to get the patient out of the hospital on time. In reality, both scenarios added one additional hospital day to the length of stay that could have been saved by meeting the discharge date. With long lengths of stay, inertia can quickly pile on extra days—especially in hospitals with high case-mix indexes and large populations of patients who have complex medical and social challenges. Paying attention to buffer consumption can help guard against the inertia of extended lengths of stay.

Multidisciplinary Rounds: The Inpatient Huddle

In Buffer Management, the color of the buffer (green, yellow, red, black) acts as a universal signal that keeps resources on the same page about a patient's progress. In fact, the buffer helps coordinate care on several levels:

- At the individual patient level, we can compare buffer consumption to the tasks that still need to be completed before discharge. Staff members can determine if the patient is on track to meet the anticipated discharge and if they need to spend more time with the patient.
- At the unit or service level, we can compare the patient's buffer consumption to the buffer consumption of other patients to prioritize activities. Patients whose buffers are fully consumed (black) need to be expedited; buffers in red, yellow, and green thirds are then prioritized in that order.
- At the system level, we can compare buffer consumption among all the hospital's patients to track the hospital from a high-level flow perspective. This tracking will provide data on how many patients are discharged on time and how many patients have delayed discharges.

A buffer report, which is a high-level chart of how much green, yellow, red, and black exists within a system, is an effective way to track multiple patients. The buffer report can reflect flow at the level of an individual provider, a unit, a specific service (e.g., elective orthopedic surgery), or the entire hospital; it can even collect data on a healthcare system or geographic region.

Buffer consumption enables a team to coordinate and prioritize all the activities that go into treating a patient; however, this degree of synchronization necessitates a template for direct communication among the resources. For example, if you are the surgeon, you own a piece of the patient's postoperative care. You know how to execute your responsibilities, but you don't necessarily know how the patient is progressing in physical therapy or whether nursing has determined the patient to be capable of wound care and performing activities of daily living. We will now return to huddles, and specifically multidisciplinary rounds (MDRs), to provide the template for coordinated team care.

In MDRs, all the stakeholders in a particular unit come together to review the patient list. They review the status (green, yellow, red, black) of each patient, and team members each share whether or not they are on track with their responsibilities for each patient. If the patient is not on track to meet the anticipated discharge date, the team can create and execute a plan to bring the patient back on target. Unless a complicated issue arises, each patient should take no more than a couple of minutes to review. Some stakeholders, such as charge nurses or social workers, are responsible for enough patients in a unit that they may need to stay for the entire meeting; stakeholders who have only a subset of patients, such as physicians or bedside nurses, can leave after discussing their patients.

In summary, we can follow an individual patient's status to determine if that patient is on track to discharge as expected. We can use buffer reports to see how efficient a hospital unit is at patient flow, or we can use buffer reports to see a snapshot of the overall health of a hospital. Care teams meet every day in MDRs to discuss the progress of their patients and coordinate resources to ensure patients are discharged on time. Hospital management can review buffer reports during weekly meetings to help focus attention on areas of flow that require attention.

STEP 4: ELEVATE THE CONSTRAINT

After working through the bottlenecks discussed in part 1 and implementing Buffer Management to exploit and subordinate to the constraint, we may still need to invest in additional constraint capacity. In chapter 9, we considered hiring a new physician to add capacity to the ED. Adding capacity to an inpatient unit requires a more substantial commitment—possibly building a new unit, adding a floor to the hospital, or constructing a new building! But let's not jump too far ahead; we have other strategies we can turn to first.

In chapter 5, we explored a number of strategies for elevating the bottleneck when the bottleneck was an inpatient or ED bed. Many of the same strategies are still applicable now that the inpatient bed is the constraint: turning an inpatient unit or space adjacent to the ED into an observation unit; leasing beds in a skilled nursing facility for underinsured patients; and converting a non-patient care space into a flex unit during times of higher volume, such as during flu season.

It's important to carefully consider any potential investment that aims to increase inpatient bed constraint capacity. As previously discussed, it is a costly mistake to invest in constraint capacity if subordinate resources are not prepared to support the constraint's increased capacity. We must avoid turning a nonconstraint into a bottleneck that then renders the constraint idle. For example, if we attempt to elevate the constraint by adding more inpatient beds, but we do not have adequate nursing or housekeeping staff to keep those beds clean, staffed, and ready for new patients, then the added constraint capacity will sit idle and the investment will have been a waste. If we decide to embark on a capital expansion project—for example, building another wing and adding 40 inpatient beds—we must be sure that we have adequate resources across the system to support the expansion.

Likewise, if we plan to increase constraint capacity by reconfiguring existing space into additional patient beds or by expanding inpatient bed capacity through new construction, we must make sure to build the right kind of beds. We should not build ICU beds if we need only floor beds; we should not build floor beds if beds in an observation unit would be more useful. When an inpatient bed is the constraint, elevating that constraint is a high-stakes endeavor.

STEP 5: DO NOT LET INERTIA BECOME THE NEW SYSTEM CONSTRAINT

In addition to synchronizing resources and keeping patients on track for discharge, Buffer Management is an excellent tool for continuous process improvement—the cornerstone of the fifth focusing step. After organizing all of a system's resources around the constraint, we must continuously refine the system to further improve workflow and shorten lengths of stay (ideally, surpassing national benchmarks).

If a buffer is chronically more than two-thirds or fully consumed (red or black), a process improvement project should be set up to determine the cause of the delays. If a specific activity routinely needs to be expedited or a certain resource is frequently spread too thin, we must understand why so that we can reengineer workflow to mitigate recurring delays. During daily MDRs, any instances of fully consumed buffers (black) should be logged, along with the reasons for consumption; resources that must expedite to catch up should be logged in a similar fashion. The patterns that emerge from these logs will point to one or more processes that need improvement.

Once the entire hospital has coordinated resources around the constraint, fine-tuned the constraint's performance, and institutionalized a continuous improvement process, excess constraint capacity will start to appear. At some point, the constraint will no longer be the inpatient bed; the new constraint will be external to patient care, such as marketing or community outreach (the marketplace). The hospital will be in a position to strategically grow its volumes. We can analyze potential lines of business—elective cardiac procedures, total joint replacements, oncology cases—to determine which types of cases would not only provide higher revenue relative to the demand for constraint resources but also complement the hospital's existing strengths. For example, cases that bring in the most revenue while simultaneously requiring the shortest inpatient lengths of stay are probably the most lucrative. We are in a position to chart our own course and control our own destiny—which is what playing offense is all about.

SUMMARY

- The inpatient bed is the constraint resource in an inpatient unit.
- All the activities in an inpatient unit must be coordinated to support the patient's discharge.
- As the constraint, the inpatient bed should not sit idle, nor should it perform nonconstraint tasks.
- We can track a patient's progress toward an on-time discharge by measuring buffer consumption (the buffer is time).
- By following daily buffer reports at MDRs, we can improve the synchronization of shared resources among patients.
- Buffer reports help prioritize who should receive resources first and signal when we need to expedite resources.
- Buffer reports provide a quick overview of patient flow on individual units (measured on a daily basis) and in the hospital system (measured on a weekly basis).
- If we need to elevate the constraint, we must first ensure that doing so does not turn a nonconstraint resource into a new bottleneck that would render the constraint idle.
- Tracking when and why expediting becomes necessary illuminates recurring problems in flow and provides focus for process improvement projects.

REFERENCE

Stewart, E. E., and B. C. Johnson. 2007. "Huddles: Improve Office Efficiency in Mere Minutes." *Family Practice Management* 14 (6): 27–29.

PART III

Outpatient Flow: Office Practices, Clinics, and Urgent Care Centers

THE UNITED STATES SPENDS an inordinate amount of money on healthcare: $10,739 per person in 2017. That's 28 percent more than Switzerland, the next-highest per capita spender (Sawyer and Cox 2018). Furthermore, in countries where median national incomes and median incomes per person are comparable to those of the United States, healthcare costs only 60 percent as much (Peterson-KFF Health System Tracker 2018). That's a 40 percent discount! And while the cost of healthcare in other countries is discounted, the quality certainly isn't. We get very little value for our money in terms of outcomes. While it's true that the United States prioritizes healthcare for people in their final months (i.e., pricey end-of-life care), we fall short on benchmarks that truly matter. Compared to nations with similar wealth, we have below-average life expectancy, higher pregnancy-related mortality, and higher mortality rates from preventable causes. Our infant mortality rate is the highest of any wealthy country in the world (Kamal, Hudman, and McDermott 2019).

While we spend far more than other countries do on healthcare, we simply don't get what we pay for. Most, if not all, of these important benchmarks—longevity, preventable mortality—are influenced by access to primary care. Our ability to effectively manage outpatient medicine and to provide timely outpatient care is critical: In 2016, only half of Americans who needed same-day or next-day appointments were able to get them (Peterson-KFF Health System Tracker 2016). A 2017 survey examined appointment wait times in major US cities for five areas of healthcare—family practice, obstetrics and gynecology, orthopedic surgery, dermatology, and cardiology (Merritt Hawkins 2017). Average wait times to see a provider were 29 days (family practice), 26 days (obstetrics and gynecology), 11 days (orthopedic surgery), 32 days (dermatology), and 21 days (cardiology). If you had to wait a month to see your family practice provider for an acute problem like a cough or sore throat, you would either be fully recovered by then or in the hospital and very ill. And these are minor problems compared to diabetics with high blood sugar or heart patients with uncontrolled blood pressure, none of whom have any more success accessing primary care than the patient with a cough or sore throat.

One of the main causes of lengthy wait times is provider shortages: Physicians no longer want to work in primary care. In 2019, there were just over 8,100 first-year training positions available for internal medicine programs. Only 41.5 percent of these spots were filled (Knight 2019). Pediatrics and family medicine, the two other primary care specialties, saw similar results.

This lack of interest in primary care medicine isn't surprising. Primary care providers (PCPs) face increasing patient demand and administrative burden. Each provider in a typical internal medicine practice could have between 2,000–3,000 patients and an average of 10–12 minutes allotted per patient appointment. In addition to full days spent rushing through care, PCPs must battle insurance companies for approvals, call patients to follow up on results and answer questions, complete charting, and catch up on the current medical literature. If a typical PCP was providing high-quality care to 2,000 patients, that physician could easily spend 17.5 hours every day on preventive, acute, and chronic care. For the privilege of working under these conditions, PCPs are among the lowest paid of all physicians. Consider, too, that not only do medical students graduate with an average of $200,000 of educational debt but a physician's earning potential also is delayed for years until after college, medical school, and residency. Why would physicians delay their earning potential until they are 30 years old, take on $200,000 of debt, work under pretty miserable conditions, and be paid below market for the privilege? They wouldn't. Hence the shortage of PCPs. Under the current model, primary care in the United States seems set up to fail—and with it, the health of our nation will inevitably decline.

When patients finally do get an appointment with a PCP, the day is often spent sitting in the waiting room as appointments run late and providers fall behind schedule. The former CEO where I (Chris) work once recounted that his wife would never see a doctor unless she could book the first appointment of the day. She knows that if she doesn't get that first slot, she could spend all day in the waiting room while the physicians and staff play catch-up. And her husband was the boss—of everything!

The state of our primary care system reminds me of the old Garment District in New York City. Adjacent to the once-seedy Hell's Kitchen, the Garment District has historically been associated with sweatshops and dangerous working conditions. It's also where labor activist David Dubinsky made his mark.

David Dubinsky was born in 1892, in what is now the former Soviet Union. He grew up in a working-class family: His first job was in his father's bakery. He was an early labor activist who was arrested several times for helping to organize bakers' union strikes. At 17, Dubinsky was exiled to a labor camp in Siberia. He managed to escape en route and found his way to America, ultimately ending up in New York City.

After arriving in New York, Dubinsky got a job as a fabric cutter in a garment factory. At that time, most garment workers earned minimal pay, worked long hours in unsafe conditions, went without breaks, and had no real voice. Dubinsky joined the International Ladies' Garment Workers' Union (ILGWU) and eventually became its president. He was a fierce champion of workers' rights who fought for better conditions, shorter hours, and higher wages. He successfully increased membership of the ILGWU tenfold, helped found the Congress of Industrial Organizations, and facilitated its merger with the American Federation of Labor and Congress. The AFL-CIO is now the largest federation of unions in the United States. Lyndon B. Johnson awarded Dubinsky the Presidential Medal of Freedom in 1969. David Dubinsky died in 1982, at the age of 90 (Famous People 2019).

What made Dubinsky so effective as a leader was his ability to work with management. He was seen as practical, mindful of reality, and in favor of win-win resolutions. Dubinsky once went to a few garment factory owners and asked for a wage increase for their workers. The owners told him that if they raised wages by even one penny, they would lose their competitive advantage and go out of business. Dubinsky argued that raising wages and improving conditions would actually increase productivity and make the factories more profitable. The owners agreed to let him test his theory in a handful of factories. As part of his strategy, Dubinsky hired efficiency experts to evaluate the factories' performance. Under improved conditions, the workers were able to implement the recommendations of the efficiency experts. Workers earned more money, worked fewer hours, and were able to increase their productivity. The factories Dubinsky operated became the most productive in the industry.

Dubinsky's approach has important applications to outpatient medicine and primary care. His philosophy of improving efficiency to make work better for everyone—his win-win paradigm—provides a roadmap for improving outpatient medicine and especially primary care.

REFERENCES

Famous People. 2019. "David Dubinsky: Biography." Accessed December 18. www. thefamouspeople.com/profiles/david-dubinsky-6022.php.

Kamal, R., J. Hudman, and D. McDermott. 2019. "What Do We Know About Infant Mortality in the US and Comparable Countries?" Peterson-KFF Health System Tracker. Published October 18. www.healthsystemtracker.org/chart-collection/ infant-mortality-u-s-compare-countries/.

Knight, V. 2019. "American Medical Students Less Likely to Choose to Become Primary Care Doctors." *Kaiser Health News*. Accessed December 16. https://khn. org/news/american-medical-students-less-likely-to-choose-to-become-primary-care-doctors/amp/.

Merritt Hawkins. 2017. "2017 Survey of Physician Appointment Wait Times and Medicare and Medicaid Acceptance Rates." Accessed December 16, 2019. www.merritthawkins.com/uploadedFiles/MerrittHawkins/Content/Pdf/ mha2017waittimesurveyPDF.pdf.

Peterson-KFF Health System Tracker. 2018. "Health Spending and the Economy: Country Comparison, 1970–2017." Accessed December 16, 2019. www. healthsystemtracker.org/indicator/spending/health-expenditure-gdp/.

————. 2016. "Health System Dashboard." Accessed December 16, 2019. www. healthsystemtracker.org/indicator/access-affordability/4578-2/.

Sawyer, B., and C. Cox. 2018. "How Does Health Spending in the US Compare to Other Countries?" Peterson-KFF Health System Tracker. Published December 7. www.healthsystemtracker.org/chart-collection/health-spending-u-s-compare-countries/.

CHAPTER 11

Understanding the Outpatient Setting

OBJECTIVES

- Define the outpatient setting
- Identify current problems in the outpatient setting
- Introduce constraint management to address outpatient problems

---

OUTPATIENT MEDICINE ENCOMPASSES a host of services including primary and specialty care. Primary care is traditionally provided by physicians (and now, more frequently, physician assistants and nurse practitioners, collectively referred to as advanced practice practitioners) trained in family practice, internal medicine, or pediatrics (obstetrics and gynecology is also considered primary care, depending on the practice focus). Primary care is usually delivered in an office or clinic setting. Specialty care is also typically delivered in an office or clinic setting and is provided by physicians who are trained in a more focused discipline, such as cardiology, gastroenterology, neurology, orthopedics, or ophthalmology. Urgent care centers are primarily staffed by advanced practice practitioners; however, emergency physicians and, less often, primary care and specialty providers may work in urgent care centers.

While the problems and inefficiencies of inpatient and outpatient medical care do overlap, the outpatient setting has some unique challenges. Patients typically have to wait days, weeks, or months to book an appointment; a patient can spend hours at the office on the day of the appointment; and high-demand appointment slots go empty if patients arrive late, cancel at the last minute, or simply skip their appointments without warning.

Providers are often forced to choose between efficiency and thorough patient care. On the one hand, they can be flexible with their schedules and spend as much time as is necessary with each patient; the downside to this approach is that it can significantly delay appointment start times throughout the day. Alternately, providers can adhere to a strict schedule and start appointments on time so that they don't keep patients waiting; the downside to this approach is that providers do not have extra time to spend with a patient if something unexpected or unplanned comes up during the appointment. Some physicians in large practices or hospital systems are under pressure to schedule patient appointments only 15 minutes apart.

PCPs often have very tight schedules that do not have room for walk-in, same-day, and next-day appointments. At the same time, physicians want to accommodate patients who need immediate attention instead of directing them to go elsewhere (urgent care centers, EDs). Patients who do end up in an urgent care center or ED often need PCP follow-up appointments anyway, which leads to multiple visits, additional wait times, additional crowding in primary care clinics, and more expensive medical bills.

Finally, many physicians feel pressure to add resources to their practices that will both expand their service offerings and ensure timely appointments for their patients. At the same time, however, there are also pressures to keep expenses and resource expansions to a minimum.

The challenge, then, is to find the best approach for managing all of these concerns, many of which conflict directly with one another. Exhibit 11.1 summarizes these conflicting concerns.

Exhibit 11.1: Key Concerns of an Outpatient Medical Practice

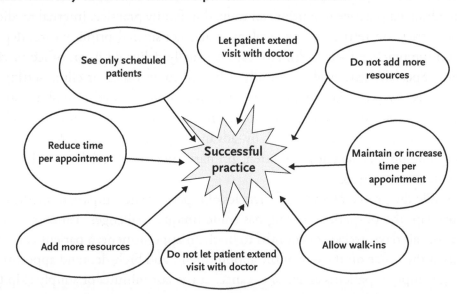

COORDINATING RESOURCES

Any solution that resolves the pain points of outpatient medicine must improve working conditions, quality of service, and patient flow; such a solution must also be financially sustainable. As we discussed in our ED and inpatient use cases in chapters 9 and 10, respectively, a system's output is a function of how well its critical resources are optimized, and the key to optimization is resource coordination. The physician's patient schedule is a great example of how resource coordination can optimize output.

We know that long wait times—both to get an appointment and to be seen on the day of the appointment—can be problematic for patients. Providers often feel rushed as daily appointments run behind schedule. At the same time, offices frequently have both last-minute patient cancellations and no-shows as well as the occasional random empty slot. Providers cannot be productive when these events occur. The net result is that providers either struggle to play catch up or sit idle, wasting time. Inefficient coordination leads to physicians who are running behind, keeping patients waiting, rushing through patient visits, and ironically, sporadically sitting idle.

Remember that most systems have a constraint resource, the predominant or critical resource that determines the system's output. This constraint is the control point that focuses system coordination: In an orchestra, it's the conductor; in a classroom, it's the teacher; in football, it always has been and always will be Joe Montana. In most primary and specialty outpatient clinics, the provider is the constraint.

Having identified the constraint of an outpatient clinic, we can now implement TOC to coordinate resources around the constraint, thereby improving flow through the clinic, providing better service to patients, and improving the providers' quality of life. We will move through implementation in three phases:

- Phase 1: Gain momentum
- Phase 2: Stabilize the system
- Phase 3: Design a continuous improvement process

In phase 1 (gain momentum), we will look at typical outpatient-clinic problems through the lens of the 5FS, using the provider as the constraint. The goal of phase 1 is to gain rapid performance improvement by exploiting and subordinating to the constraint. The central assumption is that the output of the entire system can be increased by better management of the constraint capacity. In phase 2 (stabilize the system), we will establish a formal system to operationalize and maintain the gains made in phase 1 and to position the system for further improvements. The goal of the second phase is to stabilize the system by developing processes for coordination, including a priority-setting mechanism, that aid in execution. We will employ DBR and Buffer Management in phase 2. In phase 3 (design a continuous improvement process), we further improve the system's performance by analyzing any delays we identified in phase 2. We can collect data on the reasons for those delays, for example, and use the data to design targeted improvement projects. We will look more closely at all three phases in subsequent chapters.

SUMMARY

- Outpatient care has unique challenges, including long wait times for patients to get appointments, overworked providers who have little time for each patient, and long delays as appointments run late and providers fall behind schedule.
- Clinic schedules usually have little flexibility to accommodate drop-ins or same-day appointments.
- In an outpatient clinic, the constraint or critical resource is the provider.
- Coordinating all of the clinic's resources around the constraint can improve flow and increase productivity.
- Implementing change to improve outpatient flow moves through three phases: gain momentum (phase 1), stabilize the system (phase 2), and design a continuous improvement process (phase 3).

CHAPTER 12

Phase 1: Gaining Momentum

OBJECTIVES

- Understand why the physician is the constraint in an outpatient setting
- Revisit the 5FS in an outpatient scenario
- Apply full kit to the outpatient setting

IN CHAPTER 11, WE established that TOC implementation in an outpatient setting consists of three phases. Phase 1 requires gaining momentum to promote improved workflow. The goal in phase 1 is to rapidly improve a system's performance by exploiting and subordinating to the critical resource or constraint. In the outpatient clinic setting, the provider is the constraint.[1] Let's now look at patient flow in the clinic setting using the 5FS.

Step 1: Identify the Constraint

The fundamental rules about bottlenecks apply to constraints as well. An hour of idle time for the constraint is an hour of idle time for the entire system. The cost of an hour lost on the constraint is the cost of an hour lost for the entire system. The constraint determines flow, and, as illustrated in exhibit 12.1, the constraint's rate of production dictates the system's rate of production.

In exhibit 12.1, flow through the system is represented by water flowing through pipes, which is analogous to patients moving through a clinic. Different resources in the system have different capacities, represented by the lettered sections (A–E), through which water must pass. The constraint is the resource that

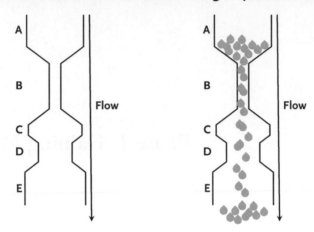

dictates how quickly or slowly the system flows. If we can make the constraint (B) produce at a higher rate, then the productivity of the entire system will increase.

Even though we have already determined that the provider is the constraint in the office or clinic setting, let's use the first focusing step to confirm our conclusion. The constraint is the most critical or predominant resource in a system; it may or may not be the bottleneck. The constraint is the resource that is the most complex, most utilized or busiest, most expensive, hardest to replace, or most difficult to add capacity to. It must make sense for the system as a whole to synchronize activities around the resource that is chosen as the constraint. It wouldn't make sense, for example, for the constraint to be the receptionist or the scheduling calendar.

In the clinic setting, the provider fits the bill. The provider is likely the most expensive resource, the most difficult to replace, and the busiest (especially with a practice of 2,000 or more patients). It would be more difficult to add providers than to add other positions. To double-check our reasoning, imagine improving flow through the constraint resource. For example, we could schedule twice as many patients on the calendar, but we still wouldn't be able to see more patients in the clinic. The scheduling calendar is therefore not the constraint. However, if the provider could see twice as many patients in the clinic, flow through the entire system would improve! The provider makes sense as the constraint.

Step 2: Exploit the Constraint

The second focusing step requires us to identify idle time for the provider and decide how to organize the day to optimize the provider's time. Similar to our prior discussions on the second focusing step, an outpatient clinic provider who sits idle or performs tasks that could be accomplished by someone else—an assistant, a tech, a nurse, the patient—is not being exploited. Remember our accountant, Joe?

Imagine yourself as the physician in an outpatient clinic: How much time do you spend doing things that someone else could do? How many times are you interrupted during the day? How often are you waiting for a patient to be ready? How often are you looking for something that is missing? What percentage of the time do you have no-shows or cancellations? How much time do you spend on activities that could be automated? If you were to add up all this idle time, would it be enough to see an extra patient or two each day? What would be the impact in a week or a month?

To reduce or eliminate idle time for the constraint, we need first to develop a strategy to exploit the constraint, then, in the next focusing step, have everyone else subordinate their activities to support the constraint. Exploiting the constraint requires determining

- which tasks can be done only by the constraint and which can be offloaded to someone else;
- how we can reduce the number of interruptions to the constraint;
- how we can prepare patients so that they use time with the physician effectively;
- how we can minimize empty appointment slots;
- how to manage the constraint's scheduling restrictions; and
- how to schedule an appropriate mix of appointments—new patients, established patients, acute concerns, chronic concerns.

Step 3: Subordinate Everything Else to the Decision Made in Step 2

Now that we have identified the constraint and decided on a mode of operation for exploiting the constraint, we must establish how to synchronize the clinic's resources to support the activities of the constraint. We must determine a strategy for execution. We must reengineer clinic workflow to maximize the constraint's effectiveness by optimizing the activities of the clinic physician. Subordinating to the constraint should ensure that the provider is always busy, performing only constraint-level tasks, and interrupted minimally.

We begin subordination by mapping out the physician's typical daily work-flow. After doing so, we should look for steps that can be offloaded to someone else in the office—for example, making follow-up phone calls, scheduling patient tests and referrals, corresponding with insurance companies, ordering supplies, and phoning in prescriptions. The clinic's medical assistants can take over chart-ing duties to augment the provider's capacity (the clinic can also invest in hiring scribes, but that investment is more of an elevation rather than a subordination). The clinic should contact patients, by telephone, email, or text message, to confirm their appointments. Confirmation should be done early enough that the clinic has time to book another patient in the event of a cancellation. Reconfirming with a final reminder the night before the appointment is also useful, as is maintaining a list of patients who are amenable to coming in on very short notice when last-minute cancellations or no-shows do occur.

Perhaps the most effective way to subordinate to our outpatient constraint is by implementing full kit. The foundation of full kit is the idea that everything needed to complete a given task is present before the task begins. In the clinic setting, full kitting minimizes the time that the constraint spends looking for equipment, searching for a chart or a missing lab result, or going to the wrong patient room. It is especially helpful to establish who in the clinic will be responsible for full kitting and to embed full kit assembly into that person's job description.

A full kit can be built around the physician's workflow, especially those activities that involve touch points with a patient. Full kitting for the clinic physician may include

- a questionnaire that patients fill out before seeing the physician, summarizing the reason for the appointment and any concerns or specific questions the patient would like to address;
- a preliminarily interview with the patient prior to seeing the physician to help the patient focus on the specifics of the appointment;
- ensuring that the physician sees the correct patient, in the correct room, at the correct time;
- completing all tests and confirming that patients have received any necessary referrals prior to the appointment;
- updating the patient's chart with relevant information, test results, and correspondence before the physician sees the patient;
- setting up supplies and instruments that the physician might need during the appointment; and
- placing every patient in a gown.

Many years ago, I (Danilo) took my wife to an urgent care center for stitches after she cut her finger in the kitchen. When we got in to see the doctor, there was a suture kit set up and waiting for him. However, as the doctor was about to start suturing, he realized that an important piece of the kit was missing. He swore, apologized, and promised to return in a minute. When he returned, however, he noticed another piece that was missing from the kit, and left again. Each time he came back in the room, he noticed something else was missing. After 45 minutes, five of which were spent actually repairing the cut, he finished up and apologized one more time. This experience is not atypical.

An outpatient clinic can make use of several different types of kits: a kit of new patient intake paperwork, a kit of sterile instrument sets for performing simple outpatient procedures, and a kit of standardized information to give to patients and their families. We can even supply patients with a finishing kit that contains everything they will need after the clinic visit, such as clinical summaries, instructions for what to do between visits, updated medication lists, and upcoming appointments.

We can extend the concept of a full kit to tasks that a patient needs to do before being seen by the constraint. For instance, a patient scheduled for a colonoscopy needs to complete a bowel prep and may need medical screening by a PCP before undergoing the procedure. Outpatient surgery centers should have, for every patient, preoperative kits that include lab and imaging results, clearance for surgery from the PCP or cardiologist, a signed consent form, preoperative evaluation by anesthesia, and insurance approval. The kit may need to be checked several times prior to the day of surgery to ensure that it is complete, especially since it is costly, both to patients and to the surgery center, to cancel at the last minute. Having a complete preoperative kit ensures that patients are ready for their procedures as scheduled.

We'll reiterate that for a full kit strategy to work, one person (per department) should be accountable for ensuring that kits are complete and properly dispensed. Ideally, a team will standardize processes, create checklists, and package kits so that they are easy to manage. The process should be documented and monitored to identify areas for improvement.

By its very nature, an outpatient clinical practice will involve some degree of multitasking, and interruptions are an inevitable part of multitasking. Interruptions must be kept to a minimum, however, to ensure optimal use of the constraint's time. A "teamlet" model (Bodenheimer and Laing 2007), in which a physician and one or two assistants take care of patients as a team, can facilitate both implementing full kit and minimizing interruptions. The assistant(s) can help with preliminary tasks that do not need to be done by the physician, such as identifying the purpose of the visit, obtaining a history of the present illness or condition, confirming the patient's current medications, and educating the patient regarding what to expect during the visit. An assistant can also help with documenting visits, ordering tests, and sending in prescriptions. After the physician's portion of the encounter is complete, the assistant can conduct a debriefing with the patient to reemphasize important points, review medications and discharge instructions, schedule follow-up appointments, and answer questions. This model can increase the capacity of the constraint, thereby improving patient flow. Using assistants also gives patients more attention, which improves patient satisfaction and minimizes future preventable problems (e.g., not understanding instructions, noncompliance with medications, missing future appointments).

Physicians can also begin to improve their workflow by keeping a daily log of interruptions as they occur. These data can determine which types of interruptions are most common and which interruptions most negatively impact flow; subsequently, the team can take corrective actions to minimize interruptions. Some recurring issues can be addressed by changing workflow. For example, any question for the physician that does not need an immediate answer could be written down for the physician to address at a more convenient time, usually later in the day. The patterns that emerge from the data will inform workflow changes and eliminate common, recurring interruptions.

Step 4: Elevate the Constraint

Once we have optimized the constraint, we may still need to add capacity to the constraint resource. If the clinic has too many patients per provider or wants to grow its patient volumes beyond current capacity, then it is time to consider measures such as extending clinic hours or hiring more providers.

Since the constraint is, by definition, the resource around which all other resources are synchronized, we must ensure that the nonconstraint resources have sufficient excess capacity to accommodate an increase in constraint capacity. If we hire another provider so that the clinic can accommodate more patients, we need enough support staff, clinic space, and supplies to handle the increase in patient volume. Imagine a scenario in which we invest in another provider (the most expensive, most complex, most highly trained resource in the system) only to have that provider sitting idle because there aren't enough receptionists to call ahead and confirm appointments or to check patients in when they arrive. We have turned a nonconstraint resource into a new bottleneck and wasted the resources spent on the extra constraint capacity. One of the advantages of constraint management is that it provides clarity when considering investment in additional hires or other resources!

If we have enough support staff, enough rooms, and enough pizza in the break room, we're ready to add constraint capacity. Adding provider hours does not necessarily mean hiring more physicians, however; we have alternatives to consider first. If there is a spike in demand for outpatient care during mornings or evenings, we could extend the clinic's hours of operation. We could shift the current provider schedule earlier or later in the day and fill the remaining hours with an additional part-time provider. Instead of an additional physician, we could hire an advanced practice provider to increase hours; using an APP has the benefit of elevating the constraint with a resource that costs less than a physician does.

Step 5: Do Not Let Inertia Become the New System Constraint

We won't belabor the point, but suffice it to say: Don't get lazy. Let's look at a case study (adapted from Bacelar 2019).

CASE STUDY

A retinal imaging unit supports ophthalmologists who need to order two types of imaging exams: fundus photography and fluorescein angiography. The unit is staffed by an ophthalmologist, a medical assistant, and a nurse. The facility is open in the afternoons and can accommodate only 12 scheduled patients and two same-day appointments each day. The facility chronically runs late, is often unable to see all of the scheduled patients for the day, and has a growing backlog of appointments. Patients are often late or don't show up to their appointments. The physician frequently has to wait while patients are prepared for their studies. The facility needs to improve its customer service and increase productivity. In its current state, there are no funds available to hire more staff or extend the facility's hours.

Applying the 5FS, what is the constraint? When might the constraint sit idle?

How could the facility's workflow be subordinated to improve productivity?

The center in this case study implemented TOC to improve performance and increase output. The team selected the physician as the system constraint. To exploit the constraint, the layout of the facility was modified so that the physician always had a patient prepped and ready to be seen. One of the main modifications was to place three chairs next to the examination area. A medical assistant was responsible for making sure there were always patients in those chairs (a patient buffer).

Patients were scheduled to arrive, five at a time, 30 minutes before their appointments (a time buffer). The first five patients would arrive at 1:30 p.m. for the 2:00 p.m. appointment; the doctor was scheduled to arrive at 2:00 p.m. This change guaranteed that at least one or two patients were prepped and ready by the time the constraint arrived. Five more patients were expected at 2:30 p.m. and another five patients at 3:30 p.m. Once patients arrived, they were prepped according to standard procedure. Some preparatory steps were completed by the assistant and some by the nurse. Up to three patients were then seated in the chairs next to the examination area. Full kitting was employed to prepare, organize, and sequence the patient's medical records, further minimizing idle time at the constraint. These actions enabled the center to increase its throughput by 25 percent, seeing 15 scheduled patients instead of 12. As the system stabilized, the constraint was able to accommodate three additional scheduled appointments (18 in total, or a 50 percent improvement from the initial 12) and three more same-day appointments (5 in total, a 150 percent improvement from the original 2). The changes were made without adding additional resources or jeopardizing the quality of service.

SUMMARY

- The goal of phase 1 is to get rapid improvements in performance by exploiting and subordinating to the constraint.
- The constraint is the resource that is the most critical or predominant resource in a system. In an outpatient clinic or office setting, the provider is the constraint.
- The constraint determines flow through the entire system.
- To optimize flow, all resources in a system must be coordinated by or synchronized to the pace of the constraint.
- To effectively exploit and subordinate to the constraint, the physician must always be kept busy, perform only constraint-level activities, and be minimally interrupted.
- Employing full kitting is one of the most effective ways to subordinate to the constraint in a clinic setting.
- Before adding capacity to the constraint, there must be sufficient excess capacity in all nonconstraint resources to accommodate the increase in volume that will accompany an increase in constraint capacity.
- Don't get lazy.

NOTE

1. The provider may not be the constraint in a nonclinical outpatient setting. For instance, in an imaging center, the constraint is most likely the imaging equipment itself.

REFERENCE

Bacelar, G. 2019. "How a Doctor Implemented TOC and Improved His Ophthalmology Practice by 50% in a Few Weeks." Video presentation at the 17th Annual TOCICO International Conference, Chicago, June 14–17.

Bodenheimer, T., and B. Y. Laing. 2007. "The Teamlet Model of Primary Care." *Annals of Family Medicine* 5 (5): 457–61.

CHAPTER 13

Phase 2: Stabilizing the System

OBJECTIVES

- Operationalize the gains made in phase 1, and set the system up for further improvements
- Develop a system to coordinate resources around the constraint
- Develop a priority-setting mechanism to aid in executing the system of coordination
- Learn to apply DBR and Buffer Management to an outpatient setting

---

I (DANILO) HAVE two grown daughters. One recently finished graduate school in biochemistry, and the other completed her undergraduate degree in engineering. When they started school, my wife and I had the "pleasure" of driving both daughters to their respective colleges. One college (let's call it college A) used a completely different approach to drop-off than the other (college B) did. College B sent parents a letter stating that incoming freshmen could be dropped off on one specific day, anytime between 9:00 a.m. and 6:00 p.m. We felt that the best time to drop off our daughter and her personal belongings would be as early in the morning as possible, to beat the rush (kind of like the CEO's wife vying for the first appointment of the day). Of course, when we arrived promptly at 9:30 a.m., there was already a long line of families simultaneously trying to unload their kids' stuff. Despite arriving early, I saw that we would have to wait at least an hour and a half to drive up to the dorm entrance. Our only other option was to park the car a long way from the dorm and lug all her things on foot (unless we wanted to get in the car, drive back home, and sign her up for an online degree).

It should have been a quick task to bring our daughter's personal belongings up to her room—instead, we were there for several hours.

My other daughter received a letter from her university, college A, that provided a specific arrival time for dorm move-in. There was a 30-minute window around the arrival time, and college A's letter stated that if a family came earlier than their arrival window, they would have to wait until their specified time to unload. If they arrived late, the student would have to wait until the end of the day to unload. When my wife and I arrived with our daughter at her dorm, there were only three cars ahead of us, and our wait was only about five minutes long. When we pulled up to the front of the dorm, a group of volunteers helped us unload our car and moved all my daughter's belongings to a staging site inside the building. Once our car was unloaded, the team leader gave us a map and a parking pass. Within a few minutes, we had parked the car and returned to the dorm, where the university had carts available to help families move belongings from the staging area to the dorm rooms. The entire experience took less than 45 minutes.

Whether knowingly or not, college A approached dorm move-in according to the scheduling principles of DBR. Scheduling resources to optimize the output of a system is complex. The challenge is to create a plan that can not only keep everything on track but also withstand the inherent variability and unexpected problems that inevitably arise in every system. DBR is a scheduling process focused on improving flow by limiting the release of raw materials into a system to support a selected critical resource. The objective of the DBR methodology is to create a schedule that ties the release of new product to the pace of the constraint (that pace is referred to as the drum). To maximize the utilization of the constraint, buffers are put in place to protect it from any variability. DBR avoids giving the constraint resource significantly more tasks than the constraint can work on, and it also ensures that the constraint always has enough work to stay busy—the constraint never sits idle for lack of new work. The mechanism to control the release of work into the system is called the rope. DBR reduces the chaos that accompanies having excessive works-in-process, making it easier to navigate the system and to monitor operations. DBR also minimizes the amount of multitasking that the constraint has to do, protects the constraint against interruptions, and helps reliably predict how long it will take to complete work.[1]

Let's review DBR in the context of Danilo's college dorm scenario. We can think of the space in front of the dorm where people drop off students' belongings—the curb space—as the constraint. Curb space is the constraint because it controls how many families can drop off belongings at a time. The drum is the schedule created by college A, in which families are assigned a specific time to arrive at the constraint; a limited number of students are scheduled in any given time frame. By setting this schedule based on the constraint's capacity, the school ensures that there are only as many families arriving at the dorm as can fit along the curb. The drum is protected by a buffer, which in this case is the allocation of a certain number of students in the half-hour window (there are a few more families scheduled at a time than there is available curb space in case there is a no-show). The buffer prevents any time delays that may render the constraint idle. The rope is the mechanism that keeps everyone's work synchronized to the pace of the drum. Only students with the correct time in their schedule can access the curb to offload their belongings. The number of families at the constraint is strictly limited at any given time, and volunteers direct cars to drive away from the constraint as soon as they have been unloaded. Both of these actions minimize chaos by limiting the inventory (works-in-process) that could pile up at the constraint. In other words, college A is choking the amount of work released into the system. The volunteers keep families moving at a desirable pace, which is equivalent to exploiting the constraint, by keeping parents and students on task instead of allowing them to talk to friends or look around before moving their cars away from the constraint. The constraint is always busy, and the next family ready to unload their vehicle is ready and waiting as soon as curb space becomes available.

We know that the critical resource or constraint determines the speed of the entire system; therefore, it needs to determine the speed at which upstream products, or works-in-process, are delivered to the constraint. If the constraint slows down, there must be a signal upstream to slow or stop the release of additional product. If the constraint speeds up, there must likewise be a signal upstream that releases more product to keep up with the constraint's demand (without overwhelming the constraint). The rope ties the release of additional product to the constraint's pace and protects the constraint from being overloaded. The rope is also designed to ensure that buffers are not too long, too short, or excessive. Since all systems have variability that needs to be managed, we can protect the system by adding strategic buffers. They act like shock absorbers in a car, protecting the schedule from "bouncing around" too much. As we've seen in several earlier examples, buffers can be based on different factors:

- Time
- Stock
- Patients

A *time buffer* ensures that any activities that prepare a product for the constraint occur early enough that the product will not be delayed in reaching the constraint. In a *stock buffer*, we ensure vital resources that feed into the constraint do not run out so that the constraint stays productive, similar to our discussion of full kitting. A *patient buffer* is created by strategically placing patients in a location that minimizes idle time at the constraint. Examples of patient buffers include the number of patients in the waiting room or the number of patients in an exam room. While not all resources need to be buffered, those responsible for keeping the constraint busy certainly do.

DBR IN AN OUTPATIENT SETTING

Remember (as if we'd let you forget) that in an outpatient setting such as a clinic, the provider is the constraint resource. Patients flow through the clinic at the speed at which the provider sees them. If we apply DBR to a clinic, then, the drum is determined by the pace at which the provider sees patients. In practice, the drum is actually the schedule of patients and is based on how long the provider needs for each type of appointment. If a provider needs 15 minutes to see an established patient for a routine visit, for example, the drum should schedule these types of patient appointments at 15-minute intervals. If a provider needs 45 minutes for other types of appointments (e.g., new patient appointments), the schedule for these types of appointments (drum) should be adjusted accordingly.

Because the constraint's time is so valuable, buffers protect the constraint from inherent variability. The typical patient may need 15 minutes for an appointment on average, but some appointments will inevitably run longer or shorter. Some patients will be either early or late, and an appointment takes no time at all if a patient doesn't show up. Variability is inherently unpredictable, so the system needs some "slack" to make sure the provider doesn't run out of patients to see.

A *time buffer* in the clinic builds in extra time between when the patient is told to arrive and when the patient's appointment is actually scheduled to begin. Asking patients to arrive early protects the constraint if the patient is running late or needs to complete paperwork before meeting with the doctor.

A *stock buffer* in the clinic ensures that there are enough supplies available—instruments, medications, and forms—so that the constraint does not run out of materials or have to spend time looking for them. With stock buffers in particular, it is helpful if the responsible person has a visual cue to signal that the buffer is running low. This is similar to the concept of *kanban* in Lean. For example, if there are reams of paper stacked up next to the copy machine, a card could be placed on top of the second-to-last ream with a reminder: ORDER MORE PAPER.

A *patient buffer* in the clinic would strategically place patients so as to minimize idle time on the constraint. Patient buffers can include the number of patients in the waiting room or in exam rooms, patients on a "rapid response" waiting list who are available on short notice, patients on the regular appointment list, patients waiting to schedule an appointment, and patients double-booked for specific times during the day.

The final element of DBR, the rope, is another type of schedule—it schedules the release of new or additional work into the system. In the clinic, the rope is essentially another schedule—the time a patient needs to show up for an appointment. The difference between the actual time of the appointment and the time that the patient needs to arrive for the appointment is the time buffer.

Scheduling too many patients will overwhelm the provider, and scheduling too few patients will leave the provider idle. If too many patients show up at once, the provider will be pressured into rushing through appointments, possibly cutting corners or missing details, in an attempt not to keep patients waiting or falling behind in the schedule. As we previously established, the rope protects the constraint from the adverse effects of releasing too much product into the system (similar to the consequences of "pull till full" in the ED). At the same time, by having a robust schedule to ensure enough patients show up at any given time, the rope helps exploit the constraint by protecting the provider from running out of patients to see.

We can represent the different kinds of buffers graphically (exhibits 13.1, 13.2, and 13.3). Exhibit 13.4 represents DBR as it applies to a clinic setting and includes the buffers from exhibits 13.1, 13.2, and 13.3. The number of steps, complexity of the system, and optimal location of each buffer will vary, but the general schema is applicable to most clinics.

In summary, when properly applied, the DBR scheduling system includes

- the drum, which sets the pace for the system by scheduling to the pace of the constraint;
- the buffers, which ensure that variability is managed and the constraint does not sit idle; and
- the rope, which chokes the release of work to prioritize the constraint's needs, minimizes chaos, and ensures that buffers are neither too big nor too small.

BUFFER MANAGEMENT IN THE OUTPATIENT SETTING

To fully utilize buffers in constraint management, we must spend a bit more time understanding how to manage them. Let's start with time buffers. The purpose of the time buffer is to start activities early enough (but not too soon) that they finish at the expected time and are completed without jeopardizing the productivity of the constraint. In an outpatient setting, we can insert a time buffer between when the patient is scheduled to arrive and when the patient is scheduled to see the doctor. Patients are often told to show up at the clinic before the actual time

Exhibit 13.1: Time Buffer

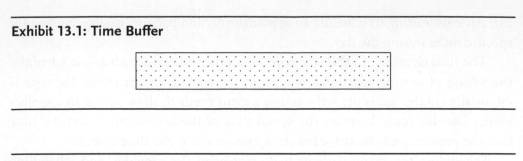

Exhibit 13.2: Stock Buffer

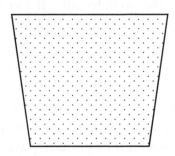

Exhibit 13.3: Patient Buffer

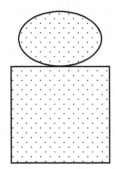

of their appointments to ensure that everything that must happen prior to seeing the physician—checking in, updating insurance information and medications, completing questionnaires, changing into a gown, providing a urine specimen—is completed before the physician enters the room. If an appointment is scheduled for 9:00 a.m. and the patient is told to come in at 8:45 a.m., the extra 15 minutes is the time buffer.[2] The time buffer generally encompasses several activities that move the patient from one point in the process to another (for example, in a hospital setting, the number of hours or days that a patient is likely to occupy an inpatient bed for a given diagnosis is a time buffer).

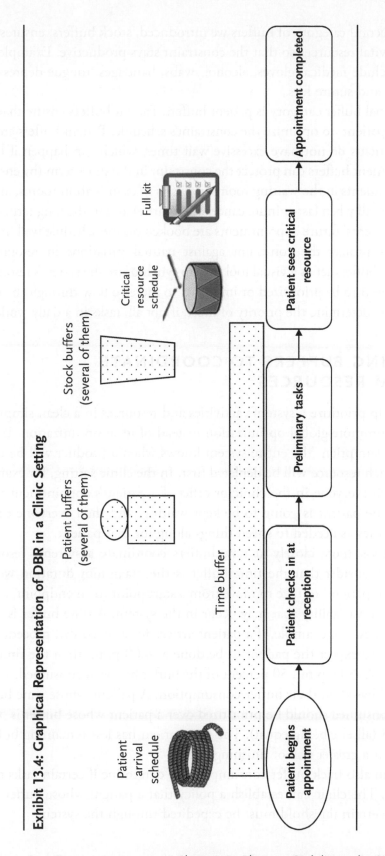

Exhibit 13.4: Graphical Representation of DBR in a Clinic Setting

Patient arrival schedule

Patient buffers (several of them)

Stock buffers (several of them)

Critical resource schedule

Full kit

Time buffer

Patient begins appointment

Patient checks in at reception

Preliminary tasks

Patient sees critical resource

Appointment completed

The second category of buffers we introduced, stock buffers, ensures the availability of vital resources so that the constraint stays productive. Examples of stock buffers include medical gloves, alcohol swabs, bandages, tongue depressors, hand sanitizers, and suture kits.

The final buffer category is patient buffers. Patient buffers ensure that there is a stream of patients to optimize the constraint's schedule. Patient buffers are designed so that patients do not have excessive wait times, which can happen if buffers are too big. Patient buffers can protect the constraint in the short term (by ensuring that there are patients in the waiting rooms, patients in examination rooms, and a list of patients to call when last-minute cancellations arise) and in the long term (by ensuring that patients' future appointments are booked on the schedule well in advance).

Buffers protect the constraint against natural variations in resources. More important, buffers act as a visual tool to help synchronize the system's resources when activities need to be prioritized or improved to increase flow through the system. In fact, buffers determine the priority of most, if not all, tasks in a daily workflow.

TRACKING BUFFERS TO COORDINATE SYSTEM RESOURCES

Buffers help prioritize a system's activities and resources in a clear, simple fashion; they also promote global optimization instead of local optimization. By tracking buffer consumption, the entire system knows when a product will be completed late or which resource will be depleted first. In the clinic setting, for example, buffers can tell everyone in the clinic or office if a patient's appointment is running late or if the patient is going to be kept waiting, and then everyone can modify their activities as needed to speed things along for that patient.

Let's look more closely at how buffers coordinate a system's resources and activities. Consider that the time buffer is the maximum duration we expect a product (or patient) to take to move from a start point to an endpoint, accounting for potential variability that may occur in the system. A time buffer is consumed as time passes. For example, if a patient arrives for a scheduled procedure at 2:00 p.m., and we expect the patient to be done at 4:00 p.m., then the time buffer is two hours. At 3:00 p.m., 50 percent of the buffer has been consumed. Patients are prioritized based on their buffer consumption. A patient whose time buffer is 75 percent consumed should be prioritized over a patient whose buffer is 50 percent consumed (all else being equal). The first patient has less remaining buffer and is therefore at a greater risk of finishing late.

We can also track buffer consumption to determine if certain tasks need to be expedited. The clinic can establish a policy that a patient whose buffer status has crossed a certain threshold must be expedited through the system.

We apply the same principle to stock buffers, tracking consumption of parts or materials instead of time. If the stock buffer calls for 30 units of a specific part and the buffer has 20 units left, then the buffer consumption is 33 percent. If several stock buffers need replenishment, the ones with higher buffer consumption should be replenished first.

A patient buffer ensures that the provider (the constraint) always has a next patient to see. If there are three exam rooms, each occupied by a patient ready to see the physician, then the buffer consumption is 0 percent. When one of the patients has been seen, buffer consumption is at 33 percent; when two patients have been seen, buffer consumption increases to 66 percent. As new patients are placed in exam rooms, the buffer is replenished; when all three rooms are occupied by patients ready to be seen by the physician, the buffer is back to 0 percent consumption.

Buffer Management uses a signal mechanism to easily notify everyone in the system of how much of the buffer has been consumed and, therefore, what activities should take priority or be expedited. Our color system of green (less than one-third buffer consumption), yellow (one-third to two-thirds buffer consumption, red (two-thirds to full buffer consumption), and black (full buffer consumption) quickly telegraphs to everyone in the system how much of the buffer has been consumed. If a buffer has been used up (black), the resource is empty or the patient's discharge is past due. Clinic staff can continuously monitor buffers to see how workflow is progressing at any given time. Visual tools, such as a computer display or colored stickers, can be used to communicate the status of the various resource buffers protecting the constraint.

The green, yellow, and red color code indicates the buffer status of each patient in the system. Exhibit 13.5 shows the division of the time buffer into thirds, with "G" representing green, "Y" representing yellow, and "R" representing red. When the buffer has been fully consumed, it is indicated by the color black.

Stock and patient buffers can be similarly subdivided as shown in exhibits 13.6 and 13.7, respectively. Visual tools communicate buffer status to all the system's resources.

Clinic personnel synchronize their activities around the constraint based on buffer consumption: Black buffers are prioritized over red, which are prioritized over yellow, which are prioritized over green. Stock buffer activities indicate which

---

Exhibit 13.5: Time Buffer Divided into Green (G), Yellow (Y), and Red (R) Zones

G	Y	R

Exhibit 13.6: Stock Buffer Divided into Green (G), Yellow (Y), and Red (R) Zones

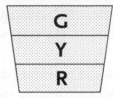

Exhibit 13.7: Patient Buffer Divided into Green (G), Yellow (Y), and Red (R) Zones

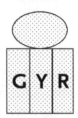

---

supplies need to be replenished first, and patient buffers ensure that patients are available at the right place and the right time.

Exhibit 13.8 depicts the cues that DBR and Buffer Management have put in place. A properly applied DBR system coupled with Buffer Management, as outlined in exhibit 13.8, can result in higher throughput, shorter wait times, and less chaotic execution. Let's look at a case study (adapted from Naik 2013).

Exhibit 13.8: Graphical Representation of DBR and Buffer Management in a Clinic Setting

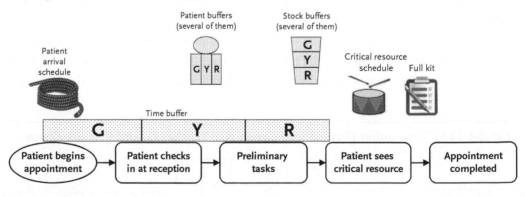

CASE STUDY

An outpatient cataract surgery center wanted solutions for improving its lead times, which it hoped would reduce chaos during times of peak volumes as well as improve patient satisfaction.

The facility wanted to reduce the overall time that a patient was at the surgery center and increase the number of patients that could be seen within a day. The waiting time for 79 percent of patients was more than two hours, which the center considered excessive. The average amount of time a patient having cataract surgery spent at the clinic (lead time) was 2 hours and 43 minutes, and the longest lead time was 5 hours and 30 minutes. Exhibit 13.9[3] outlines the high-level steps followed in the surgery center.

Exhibit 13.9: Patient Flow in Cataract Surgery Center

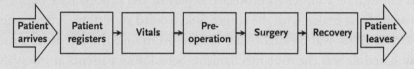

Before implementing any changes, everyone agreed that there would be no compromises to any quality measures associated with the facility or the physicians. The physicians would determine the criteria for measuring quality. Everyone also agreed that changes would not be viable if they were too expensive, compromised staff wellness, or created greater dissatisfaction among patients.

What is the system's constraint? What are some ways to exploit the constraint?

Identify the drum, buffer, and rope in the surgery center. How can DBR and Buffer Management be applied to stabilize the system?

What types of buffers could the center use to improve flow?

After many discussions, the team determined that the limiting resource in the center was the time it took a doctor to perform each surgery. Investments such as more staff, more space, or improved equipment would not improve the performance of the constraint—that is, they would not reduce the amount of time the doctor spent per patient in surgery. Therefore, the doctor was the constraint and all other activities must be subordinated.

To protect the doctor's time, the facility implemented a patient buffer. A second patient who was prepped and ready for surgery was placed in the room adjacent to the room where the doctor was currently performing surgery. When the first patient's surgery was complete, the doctor could quickly switch to the next patient without wasting time. The center also assigned a staff member the job of preparing all the necessary supplies—a full kit—one day prior to surgery. These actions were a combination of exploiting and subordinating to the constraint.

Recall that in DBR, the drum is the schedule of the constraint; it sets the pace for the overall system. The length of time needed to perform the surgery created the drum schedule. The drum schedule also had to factor in the pace of the individual physician performing surgery that day. Some doctors could perform the surgery in 10 minutes while slower ones needed 30 minutes.

Before TOC implementation, the team would have all of the morning patients arrive at the same time to ensure that there was a constant flow of patients available for the doctor. There were, however, consequences to the *en masse* arrivals. Patient wait times could be as long as five hours, which was considered unacceptable. To address this problem, the team established a time buffer of one hour. One hour provided enough of a buffer to protect the part of the process that began with the patient's arrival and ended with the surgery's scheduled start time. A new schedule for patient arrival times was created based on the drum and the one-hour time buffer. This new schedule was the rope mechanism. Scheduling patients at intervals helped reduce wait times and prevented overcrowding in the waiting room and prep areas.

A second time buffer was implemented to protect the total time the patients stayed in the system. The clinic had two hours from the time the patient arrived to when the patient should be leaving the center. Doctors and clinic staff had input on the length of the time buffer to ensure that quality of care would not be jeopardized. The team understood that some patients would consume the entire buffer (e.g., some patients with diabetes had elevated blood sugar levels, elderly patients often needed more time to recover, certain patients' eyes took longer to dilate), but they expected that 80 percent of patients would be treated within two hours.

To aid the team in Buffer Management, the two time buffers were combined. During the first 60 minutes after a patient's arrival to the clinic, the buffer status was green, and it represented the time until the patient was expected to begin surgery. Between 60 and 75 minutes, the buffer status was yellow; the team anticipated that patient surgeries would take place during this window. Between 75 minutes and 120 minutes, the patient buffer status was red; by the end of 120 minutes, the team expected that almost all patients would be discharged.[4] The staff placed colored stickers on the front of patients' folders to communicate buffer status. The color-coding helped in several ways: It kept patients flowing at a steady pace, ensuring that the physician always had prepped patients who were ready for surgery; it kept the constraint (the physician) on track while performing surgeries; and it reduced total patient treatment times. Exhibit 13.10[5] represents the surgery center's new and improved patient flow incorporating DBR.

Exhibit 13.10: Updated Patient Flow in Cataract Surgery Center

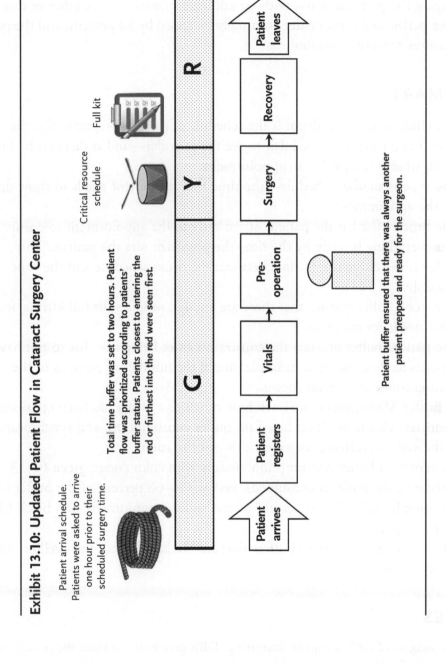

Patient arrival schedule.
Patients were asked to arrive one hour prior to their scheduled surgery time.

Critical resource schedule

Full kit

Total time buffer was set to two hours. Patient flow was prioritized according to patients' buffer status. Patients closest to entering the red or furthest into the red were seen first.

G   Y   R

Patient arrives → Patient registers → Vitals → Pre-operation → Surgery → Recovery → Patient leaves

Patient buffer ensured that there was always another patient prepped and ready for the surgeon.

After TOC implementation, the percentage of patients who waited less than two hours increased from 21 percent to 86 percent. The average lead time decreased from 2 hours and 43 minutes to 1 hour and 47 minutes. The longest wait time went from 5 hours and 30 minutes to 4 hours and 5 minutes. During its peak time, the facility was able to perform 50 percent more surgeries than it had during the previous year—without adding any staff. The number of cataract surgeries performed at the center eventually increased by 80 percent, and the quality measures remained constant.

SUMMARY

- In a clinic setting, the drum is the schedule of patients—specifically, the time that a patient is scheduled to see the provider—and is dictated by how much time is needed for an appointment.
- The rope is another schedule—the time that the patient needs to show up for the appointment.
- The time buffer has the patient arrive early to the appointment to ensure that everything is ready by the time the physician sees the patient. This buffer is the difference in time between the drum schedule and the rope schedule.
- The stock buffer ensures that there are enough supplies for full kitting and other needs for materials.
- The patient buffer protects the constraints from being idle due to not having patients ready to be seen. Examples are of the number of patients in the waiting room or in exam rooms.
- In Buffer Management, we track how much of a buffer has been consumed, prioritize what to work on based on buffer consumption, and synchronize all of the system's activities based on this prioritization.
- We represent buffer consumption visually with color codes: green (0–33 percent of the buffer is consumed), yellow (34–66 percent of the buffer is consumed), red (67–100 percent of the buffer is consumed), and black (the buffer is gone).
- We give higher priority to buffers that are black, then red, then yellow, and finally green.

NOTES

1. The origins of DBR are quite interesting. DBR gets its name from the paradigm of a group of soldiers marching in line. Let's assume the slowest soldier is somewhere in the middle of that line. The slowest soldier is the constraint and sets the pace for

how quickly all the soldiers can arrive at their destination as a unit. The soldiers behind the constraint will arrive just after the constraint (assuming that the soldiers are not allowed to pass each other in line), while the soldiers in front of the constraint will spread out as they march forward at their individual, faster paces. The idea is to identify the smallest set of controls needed to prevent the soldiers in front from spreading out as they march. To ensure all the soldiers remain together, we give the slowest soldier a drum. The drum beats at the pace of the slowest soldier and signals the pace of the constraint to the rest of the unit. Theoretically, the soldiers in front could still separate; nothing is preventing them from doing so. Therefore, we need an additional control mechanism. We tie a rope from the lead soldier to the soldier with the drum. Now the front soldier's progress is literally tied to the constraint, and the soldiers between the constraint and the lead soldier must stay together. We want to provide enough flexibility in the rope that the soldiers don't trip, so we assign a little extra rope—a buffer—to account for the variability in speed among the faster soldiers. The buffer also accounts for any variability in speed of the constraint. We now have a situation where the group of soldiers stay together using a drum, a buffer, and a rope.

2. Patients can use buffers, too. Suppose a patient is supposed to be at the clinic at 8:45 a.m. and that it takes 20 minutes to get there from home. If the patient leaves 30 minutes before the appointment just to be safe, the extra 10 minutes the patient is allowing for traffic is also a time buffer.

3. The actual flowchart of the process was a little more complicated than shown in the exhibit, but we have simplified it for clarity.

4. Note that the surgery center did not use a traditional TOC color code system, as they did not divide their buffers into thirds. However, they designed a system that satisfied their specific needs. DBR can be modified to consider the specific realities of an individual facility.

5. Even though the flowchart was simplified in exhibit 13.9, the DBR process described in exhibit 13.10 is accurate as actually implemented.

REFERENCE

Naik, D. 2013. "Applying TOC in a Leading Eye Hospital." Video presentation at the 5th International TOCPA Conference, Pune, India, April 6–7.

CHAPTER 14

Phase 3: Designing a Continuous Improvement Process

OBJECTIVES

- Develop a process to identify new or recurrent causes of significant delays
- Implement a system to focus ongoing improvement efforts
- Learn how to aggregate buffers
- Implement strategies to increase the number of available patient appointments

---

IN PHASE 1 WE applied the 5FS to identify, exploit, subordinate to, and elevate the constraint. In phase 2, we used DBR and Buffer Management to stabilize the system. We operationalized changes to ensure that we would not lose improvements over time. In the final phase of implementation, we design a process for continuous improvement to get more out of the system. Phase 3 returns to the fifth focusing step and uses Buffer Management to identify problem areas that will inform additional process improvement projects.

As patients move through the system, they wait for resources to become available. The resource that patients wait for the most is a good place to start looking for the root causes of delays. We look for delays in the system to inform future process improvement projects. Delays often manifest as buffers that are chronically depleted. For example, time buffers that are constantly more than two-thirds or completely consumed (red or black) signal that patients are repeatedly waiting for the same activity or resource(s). By tracking how often and how long patients wait—for lab work, X-rays, an exam room, or nursing tasks, for example—we can identify and prioritize where to focus our improvement efforts. For stock buffers, we want to know if certain supplies are constantly missing or frequently depleted. In terms of patient buffers, we need to be aware if the physician is frequently waiting for a patient to be placed in a room or for a patient to change into a gown. We also want to know the frequency of cancellations or no-shows and if we are able to fill open appointment slots at the last minute.

For tasks that take longer, such as filling the appointment calendar or ordering supplies, we may need to track buffer consumption over a few weeks. For shorter tasks, such as the time a provider needs to see a patient, we may be able to collect sufficient data in a day or two.

When we track delays, we are looking for recurring reasons that explain why the constraint is delayed or sitting idle. Once we have identified the causes, we create improvement projects to correct the problems:

- Frequent no-shows or cancellations?
  - Contact patients by telephone, email, or text a week before and the day before the appointment.
  - Maintain a list of patients who can come in on short notice.
  - Double-book patients during times of the day or days of the week when no-shows are most common.
  - Accept same-day and walk-in appointments at the end of the day.
- Provider spends too long with each patient?
  - Space out appointment times a bit (adjust the rope and time buffer).
  - Group similar types of appointments, so those that require less time (e.g., healthy patients who need routine checkups) are scheduled on the same day or preferentially scheduled in the morning.
  - Book longer appointments for new patients, follow-up visits after hospital discharges, and elderly patients with multiple chronic medical conditions.
- Wait times to obtain an appointment are too long?
  - Review the patient wait list to make sure everyone on the list still needs an appointment.
  - Aggregate buffers to schedule more appointment slots.
  - Extend clinic hours on select days of the week or during specific times of year.
  - Aggressively work the waitlist to fill last-minute cancellations.

AGGREGATING BUFFER TIME

A word about reducing the length of time for patient appointments: When we estimate how long a task will take, we often build in a buffer, even if we don't realize we are doing so. We expect that by adding a buffer, we prevent the task from running late. However, this strategy doesn't always work—in fact, it almost never works. A year ago, when I (Chris) talked to my editor about the deadline for this manuscript, I thought I had all the time in the world. Now, as I type these very words, it's only noon, I'm on my eighth cup of coffee, and I'm scrambling to meet my deadline—and I'm writing a book on flow!

Student syndrome and Parkinson's law are two phenomena that explain why buffers don't always protect us. Student syndrome states that regardless of how much time we have for a project, we will always wait until the last minute to start. In college, even when I asked for an extension on papers, I still found myself pulling all-nighters to finish. It's not that it took me longer than everybody else to write a paper; rather, I always found something better to do until just before the paper was due.

Parkinson's law states that no matter how long we have for a task, we will keep tweaking it up until the last minute, believing we can always make it better. Software coders are a great example: Coders always believe that a program can be written more elegantly or efficiently, documentation can be more complete, and the functionality can be more user-friendly. They will continue to work on a program until the very last minute, even if they have written a working version with plenty of time to spare.

Clinic appointments are often scheduled for longer than necessary to add a buffer and, in theory, protect against the appointments running late. However, if a patient is scheduled for 30 minutes, it is guaranteed that the appointment will use up every available second, even if it doesn't need to. Have you ever gone to the doctor and had your appointment finish early? Knowing that we tend to build in a buffer when scheduling tasks, we may have an opportunity to shorten the duration of clinic appointments, add an extra appointment slot with the time saved, and still build in a time buffer to protect against delays or appointments running late. Imagine a clinic that schedules four patient appointments before lunch, each 30 minutes long (exhibit 14.1).

Exhibit 14.1: Sample Clinic Morning Schedule Including Time Buffer

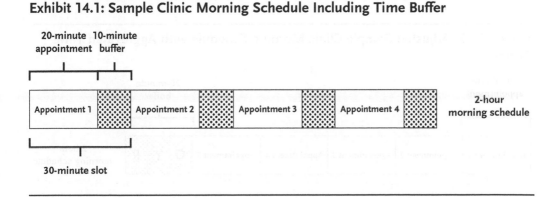

Exhibit 14.1 shows that although each appointment is scheduled for 30 minutes, the appointment itself takes only about 20 minutes. The additional 10 minutes acts as a buffer, a "safety" to protect the appointments from running late. Unfortunately, adding 10 additional minutes doesn't prevent the schedule from falling behind; it simply invites the doctor and patient to take up all 30 minutes of available time. If we shorten each appointment to 20 minutes, however, the doctor and patient will feel a sense of urgency and are less likely to waste time. If we shorten all four morning appointments, we can free up an additional 40 minutes that can be used to schedule additional patients. Leaving a small time buffer in the schedule is important, so rather than adding two more 20-minute appointments, we can add one 20-minute appointment and leave a 20-minute time buffer after the last appointment. If any of the five morning appointments run late, the staff will track the delay with our color code to signal how much of the 20-minute buffer has been consumed. Green indicates that appointments are running less than 6 minutes and 40 seconds late; yellow indicates that appointments are running between 6 minutes and 40 seconds and 13 minutes and 20 seconds late; red indicates that appointments are running between 13 minutes and 20 seconds and 20 minutes late; and black indicates that everybody is going to miss lunch. The color code lets the staff and physician know when to prioritize and expedite to get the schedule back on track. Exhibit 14.2 depicts our adjusted schedule.

Buffer aggregation can be used for outpatient clinic and office appointments, elective surgery schedules, and some radiology procedures.

SUMMARIZING THE THREE PHASES OF IMPLEMENTATION

To summarize, we begin phase 1 of implementation with a high-level understanding of the problems we currently face, the undesirable effects of those problems, and a sense of their magnitude. We consider the length of time it takes a patient

Exhibit 14.2: Adjusted Sample Clinic Morning Schedule with Aggregated Time Buffer

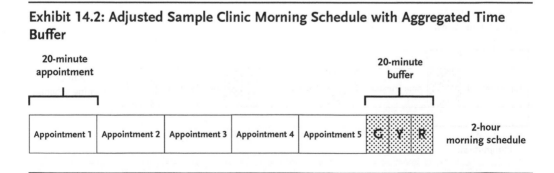

to get an appointment, the length of wait times at the office, the number of no-shows and cancellations, financial issues, times the physician is idle or performing nonphysician-level tasks, and other related issues. Then we gather momentum by obtaining quick gains in performance—to do so, we must implement the fastest and simplest tactical changes that can create rapid improvements. The 5FS help us identify the constraint, determine how to exploit the constraint, subordinate everything else to the constraint, and elevate the constraint.

In phase 2, we seek to stabilize the system by operationalizing changes through DBR and Buffer Management. We set a schedule based on the pace of the physician; add time, stock, and patient buffers to protect the physician's time from inevitable variations in the system; and implement ropes to ensure that additional patients enter the system at a pace that matches the physician's pace. This second phase requires more effort, but it also increases the probability that improvements become embedded in the clinic's operations.

Finally, in phase 3 we continue to optimize the system by establishing a process of continuous improvement and changing scheduling policies to accommodate more patients.

Let's look at a case study (adapted from Cox and Robinson 2012; Cox, Robinson, and Maxwell 2014, 2015).

CASE STUDY

A family medicine clinic is staffed by ten providers. The clinic frequently had patients who did not show up for their appointments. The office also had many unfilled appointments, especially in the summer. The physicians were often waiting for the patients to arrive or complete tasks before being seen, which resulted in excessive delays at the constraint. Physicians were frequently interrupted or had to leave patient rooms to do other tasks, exacerbating wait times and making appointments longer than necessary. The employees felt as though everyone was constantly putting out fires, which made work harder than necessary. The clinic's profits were low, and both patient and staff satisfaction were suffering. Patient flow through the clinic is represented by exhibit 14.3.

For phase 1 of implementation, list the obvious problems in the clinic. How might we use the 5FS to make rapid gains?

For phase 2 of implementation, apply DBR to the clinic's workflow map in exhibit 14.3. Where might we place buffers, and how can we use them to synchronize everyone's efforts?

(continued)

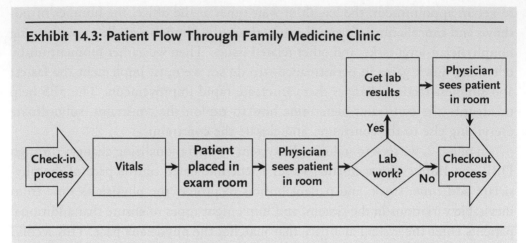

Exhibit 14.3: Patient Flow Through Family Medicine Clinic

For phase 3 of implementation, what type of data should we gather to make additional improvements, reduce areas where patients might be waiting for resources, and add available clinic appointments each day?

In phase 1, the staff compiled a list of some of the biggest, most obvious problems in the clinic. The list included inconsistencies in scheduling appointments, patient cancellations and no-shows, inefficient use of the physicians' time, long wait times, and appointments running late. The clinic then examined these problems through the lens of the 5FS. The providers were identified as the system constraint. Nonconstraint tasks were transferred from the providers to other personnel, and job descriptions were modified to reflect those changes. A provider's interruption analysis was conducted to capture the reasons for delays, and the clinic implemented changes to deal with the major reasons for disruptions. Full kits were provided so that exam rooms were equipped with everything the provider might need during a typical appointment.

Once the constraint was identified as the clinic's physicians, the clinic entered phase 2 by using DBR and implementing mechanisms to protect the constraint from variability.

As illustrated in exhibit 14.4, several buffers were added to the clinic's workflow. A time buffer of 15 minutes was put in place between when a patient was scheduled to arrive and when the patient would see the physician. In exhibit 14.4, the 15-minute time buffer appears above the arrow at the far left. The letters G, Y, and R represent the color codes of buffer consumption: green, yellow, and red, respectively. The time buffer helped the staff identify potential "no show" patients and to prioritize which patients to check in next. Patients who had been waiting 11–15 minutes (red) were prioritized over those waiting 6–10 minutes (yellow) and those waiting 1–5 minutes (green).

Exhibit 14.4: Buffers Added to Clinic Workflow

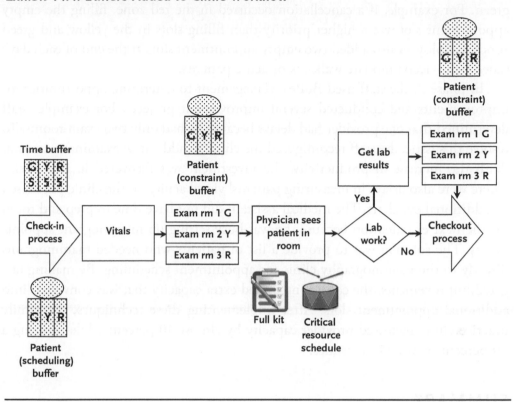

A patient buffer was implemented in front of the constraint—labeled "patient (constraint) buffer" in exhibit 14.4—to ensure that the physician never sat idle because a patient was not ready and waiting in an examination room. The patient constraint buffer was used to prioritize the activities of the personnel responsible for prepping patients to see the doctor. In the office, green indicated that the physician was seeing a patient and two more patients were prepped and waiting in exam rooms. Yellow indicated that the physician was seeing a patient, one more patient was prepped in an exam room, and one exam room was empty. Red indicated that the physician was seeing a patient and no other patients were prepped and waiting.

A second patient buffer was introduced upstream of the entire process—labeled "patient (scheduling) buffer" in exhibit 14.4—to ensure the physician had a steady stream of patients scheduled to come into the clinic and to avoid having appointment slots go unfilled. The patient scheduling buffer contained three days' worth of scheduled patients. Red represented patients scheduled for the current day, yellow for patients scheduled the next day, and green for patients scheduled for the following day. When possible, the staff scheduled new appointments based on the color code, first filling all empty slots in the red zone, then yellow, then green. For example, if a cancellation occurred in the red zone, filling the empty appointment slot was a higher priority than filling slots in the yellow and green zones. Employees also added two empty appointment slots at the end of each day's schedule to accommodate walk-ins or acute patients.

In phase 3, the staff used Buffer Management to determine opportunities for improvements and conducted several improvement projects. For example, staff determined that one provider had delays because he had only two exam rooms. To resolve this issue, the staff reconfigured the clinic to add a new examination room. With the increase in productivity, the investment was recovered in five weeks. There were also delays in measuring patients' visual acuity, so the clinic purchased an additional eye chart. The medical assistant did not have time to prep and room for the next examination because she was busy setting up mammogram appointments. The solution was to provide a list of patients who needed mammograms directly to the mammography clinic for appointment scheduling. By making targeted improvements, the constraint gained extra capacity that was converted into additional appointment slots. After implementing these techniques, the family practice clinic increased provider capacity by almost 40 percent while realizing a 29 percent increase in revenues.

SUMMARY

- In phase 3 of implementation, we seek to increase the system's performance by looking for delays in the system and then creating improvement projects to correct those delays.
- We can analyze buffer consumption patterns to quickly identify recurring delays. When buffers are repeatedly in the red or black (mostly or fully consumed), there are opportunities for process improvement involving the workflow activities responsible for consuming these buffers.
- There is typically some degree of buffer built into individual tasks, but student syndrome and Parkinson's law tell us that these buffers do not usually protect the task from taking more time than anticipated.
- By removing the buffers built into individual tasks, we can shorten the time allotted for each task. In the clinic, this means we can shorten each appointment and add more appointment slots to the schedule.
- We protect the new, shorter appointments from running over by aggregating the extra time we removed from the individual slots and adding half that amount of time back as a time buffer at the end of the schedule.
- Phase 3 is a continuous process of improvement to streamline operations, add capacity, grow volume, and increase revenue.

REFERENCES

Cox, J. F. III, and T. M. Robinson. 2012. "The Use of TOC in a Medical Appointment Scheduling System for Family Practice." Video presentation at 10th Annual TOCICO International Conference, Chicago, June 3–6, 2012.

Cox, J. F. III, T. M. Robinson, and W. Maxwell. 2015. "Unconstraining a Doctor's Office." *Industrial Engineer* 48 (2): 28–33.

———. 2014. "Applying the 'Theory of Constraints' to Solve Your Practice's Most Vexing Problem." *Family Practice Management* 21 (5): 18–22.

Epilogue

IF YOU ASK ANYONE involved in patient care or healthcare administration, they will agree that patient flow is important. It's a pretty safe, noncontroversial sentiment—but it doesn't always translate into support or action. Managing flow is hard. One strategy to garner support for improving flow is to start small. Choose projects that are easy to execute and sure to demonstrate quick successes, then leverage these successes with all your energy. Celebrate them with the team that did the work, promote them to anyone who will listen—especially the people you need to involve for your next, larger projects. Establish easy wins, and use those wins to show the value of investing in bigger, more complicated projects. Acknowledge every person who had anything to do with the win, and turn those individuals into recruiters and missionaries, spreading the gospel of flow. And never underestimate the motivational power of a pizza party.

Linking improvements in flow to financial metrics can be exceedingly helpful. At some point, you'll need hospital administration to invest resources into your work. While patient care is the top priority, it is easier to ask for resources if you can demonstrate a clear and direct return on the investment. Metrics can include reductions in time spent on ambulance diversion, reductions in rates of patients who leave the ED without being seen, decreases in inpatient lengths of stay, increases in ED admissions, and increases in elective surgeries, procedures, and overall hospital volumes. The hospital's accountant, comptroller, or CFO can provide the dollar amounts associated with these metrics. For outpatient facilities, the metrics are more straightforward: patient volumes and profits. Track your chosen metrics and their corresponding dollar amounts religiously.

TOC can be a powerful tool for improving patient flow through your hospital, ED, outpatient clinic, or medical office. Organizations have created monumental changes when TOC is used well.

There are also many organizations working hard to implement TOC that have nothing to show for it. The same can be said for Lean, Six Sigma, and any other methodology. When groups struggle to make lasting improvements, the methodology is seldom the root cause of the problem (although it is the easiest thing to blame).

Uniformly, groups that are successful have the support of their leaders. Support requires more than merely saying that flow is important; leaders must show that flow matters. Hospital leadership should provide a clear mandate that prioritizes improving patient flow.

More important, leadership must act in accordance with its mandate. People need to be rewarded for good work and held accountable for lack of progress. When flow projects fail, it is often because leaders have no presence in meetings or strategy sessions. Flow projects fail when, meeting after meeting, nobody has shown any progress on their projects and there is a lack of accountability. When leaders don't step in to find out why projects have stalled, and the projects have no sense of urgency, these projects ultimately go nowhere.

Implementation can also fail if the people tasked with improving flow aren't given sufficient time or resources to do the requisite work. Members of flow teams often have to complete their work on flow *in addition to*—not instead of—their other responsibilities. It would be far better to pause nonflow projects, reassign or cancel meetings, and give the people responsible for flow work enough time and resources to actually get the job done. How can flow be prioritized if it's item 15 on someone's task list?

Finally, Eli Goldratt used to say not to confuse an obstacle with a bottleneck. In the course of implementing TOC, we often hear excuses for why a process can't be changed or an idea can't be executed. The excuse is rarely followed by another suggestion that could work instead. People are happy with the easy "no," but "no" doesn't advance a project or promote teamwork—it just sucks the energy from the room. Doing nothing is an obstacle. An idea might not be very good, but if no one else has a better idea, then the not-very-good idea is the best one out there. It's better to go with the best idea than to sit with your thumb in your nose and do nothing.

Go forth and flow!

Additional Reading

John Kotter has written many books on leadership and change management, and a new edition of his book *Leading Change* was published in 2012. This is a phenomenal book that can be wildly helpful for managing flow teams.

For a wonderful introduction to Lean and an in-depth discussion of the Toyota Production System, Jeffrey Liker's book *The Toyota Way* is a must-read. If you are a Lean or Six Sigma practitioner and would like to know how these methodologies can be integrated with TOC, you should read *Theory of Constraints, Lean, and Six Sigma Improvement Methodology: Making the Case for Integration* by Bob Sproull. The book presents a structured process for harnessing the power of all three process improvement approaches.

Alex Knight is probably the leading expert on TOC applications in healthcare. His business novel, *Pride and Joy*, describes TOC and Buffer Management in a hospital system in England. While it specifically applies to England's nationalized healthcare system, the book's lessons about synchronizing resources, breaking down silos, and changing culture are universal and invaluable. When I (Chris) took my first job as a hospital flow director, I had not yet read his novel. Serendipitously, I had stumbled on similar ideas for Buffer Management from other sources (although at the time I didn't know that's what it was called), but I imagine our progress would have been much swifter had I read *Pride and Joy* before beginning my role.

Regardless of which methodology you ultimately land on, you'd be crazy not to devour Eli Goldratt's novel *The Goal*. The book is Goldratt's introduction of the Theory of Constraints and the five focusing steps (then read his later works for Drum Buffer Rope and Buffer Management). *The Goal* has helped me (Chris) care for more patients during my career than any medical text or clinic rotation ever could. Goldratt wrote many books, and they're all worth reading: *Critical Chain, It's Not Luck, Necessary but Not Sufficient, Isn't It Obvious?*

If you manage a clinic, you may want to read *Dentistry with a Vision: Building a Rewarding Practice and a Balanced Life* by Gerry Kendall and Gary Wadhwa.

It is written from a dentist's perspective, but the content is applicable to all kinds of private clinics who want to grow their business.

The Bottleneck Rules by Clarke Ching is a quick read that makes the reader aware of bottlenecks and identifies ways to overcome them. It presents a variation of the 5FS that can complement what we've written in *Smash the Bottleneck*.

Finally, there is a body of knowledge in TOC known as the Thinking Processes that targets decision-making for complex problems that require innovative approaches to solve them. *The Logical Thinking Process* by Bill Dettmer is an excellent reference for this subject area.

The real breakthroughs in hospital flow and operational management are most likely to come from lessons learned outside of medicine and then applied to healthcare. For example, we use the Mattel factory throughout this book because it is fairly easy to discuss concepts of flow in the context of a manufacturing plant. The concepts can then be applied to a hospital or clinic setting. It is incredibly helpful for us to learn applications outside of our professional comfort zones, and then adapt those lessons using the real-world experiences we have gained from working in our own field. To that end, check out *The Phoenix Project* by Gene Kim, Kevin Behr, and George Spafford (a business novel about TOC applications in information technology and development operations), *The Cash Machine* by Richard Klapholz and Alex Klarman (a novel about using TOC for sales management), and *Velocity* by Dee Jacob, Suzan Bergland, and Jeff Cox (a novel that explores combining Lean and Six Sigma with TOC to achieve breakthrough results in a scientific company).

Index

Note: Italicized page locators refer to exhibits.

department flow and application of, 90, 98–99, *100,* 103, 104n1; example of, 80–82; family medicine clinic and use of, 154–56; in outpatient setting, 137–38, 140. *See also* Buffers

Buffer Management, facilitating inpatient unit flow with, 107–16; do not let inertia become the new constraint, 115; elevate the constraint, 114–15; exploit the constraint, 108–9; identify the constraint, 108; subordinate everything else to the constraint, 109–14

Buffer Management, on an inpatient unit, 110–13; orthopedic surgery example, 111; sepsis example, 111–12

Buffer reports: purpose and benefits of, 113, 114, 116

Buffers, 39; benefits of, 82–83; in cataract surgery center case study, 143–44, *145*; in dorm move-in example, 135; in Drum Buffer Rope, 77, 79, 86; in emergency department flow, 93, 94; family medicine clinic workflow and, 154–56, *155*; levels of coordinated care and, 113; in outpatient setting, 136–37; patient, 135, 136–37, *138, 139,* 140, 141, 146; stock, 135–36, *138, 139,* 140, 141, 146, 149–50; time, 135, 136, 137, 138, *138, 139,* 146, 149. *See also* Buffer consumption; Buffer Management

Buffers, tracking to coordinate system resources, 140–44, 146; Drum Buffer Rope and buffer management in clinic setting, graphical representation of, 141–43, *142,* 146; patient buffer divided into green, yellow, and red zones, 141, *142*; stock buffer divided into green, yellow, and red zones, 141, *142*; time buffer divided into green, yellow, and red zones, 141, *141,* 141–42

Buffer time: aggregating, 150–52, 156

Cancellations, 123, 127, 128, 150, 153, 156

Capacity: adding, to emergency department beds, 61–62; adding, to inpatient beds, 58–60; nonbottleneck resources and, 59

Care coordination resources, 61

Case studies: ambulance diversion, reasons for, 20, *21,* 22; elevating the bottleneck, 63; family medicine clinic patient flow, 153–56, *154, 155*; inertia as new bottleneck, 66–67; inpatient bed as bottleneck resource, 32; operational measurements, 8; patient flow in cataract surgery center, *143,* 143–44, *145,* 146; subordinating everything to the bottleneck, 53, 54; subordinating workflow to improve productivity, 131

Cash Machine, The (Klapholz and Klarman), 162

Cataract surgery center: patient flow in, *143,* 143–44, *145,* 146

Centers for Medicare & Medicaid Services: patient flow performance measure, xx

Changed constraints / do not let inertia become the new system constraint (step 5), 71; continuous process improvement and, 115; gaining momentum and, 131–32; improving emergency department flow, 103

Charge nurse: emergency department, 94

Chest pain: order set for patients with, 97

Ching, Clarke, 162

Constraining resource, xxiii, 72, 73, 89, 123, 124, 125, 132

Constraint management, xxv, 71; advantages of, 130; works-in-process minimized with, 75–76. *See also* Drum Buffer Rope

Constraint management, emergency department flow improved with, 87–105; do not let inertia become the new constraint, 103; elevate the constraint, 101–2, *102*; exploit the constraint, 89–90, *91, 92,* 92–93; identify the system's constraint, 88–89; optimizing flow, considerations for, 88; subordinating everything else to the constraint, 93–99, *100*

Constraints, 66; bottlenecks vs., 71; in dorm move-in example, 134; identifying, 71, 72–73; pace of, 72, 76; reminders about, 88; understanding definition of, 71. *See also* Bottlenecks

divided into, 141, *142*; stock buffer divided into, 141, *142*; tax preparation example, *81,* 81–82; time buffer divided into, 141, *141*

Grey's Anatomy (television show), xvii

Hallway beds: capacity and, 59

Healthcare: full kitting in, 83; operational measurements in, 6–9

Healthcare delivery system: goals in, 13; overcrowding endemic in, xix, xxv

Healthcare expenditures: in United States, 117

Hoarding patients, 55

Holter monitors, 60

Hospital patient flow: process map of, *16*

Hospitals: dependent events and statistical fluctuations in, 46; football analogy for, 69–70; inventory in, 6; operating expense in, 7; overcrowding in, financial costs of, xix–xx, xxv; throughput in, 6, 7

Hospital settings, elevating the bottleneck in, 58–64; adding capacity to emergency department beds, 61–62; adding capacity to inpatient beds, 58–60; reducing demand for emergency department beds, 62–64; reducing demand for inpatient beds, 60–61

Hospital systems, subordinating to the bottleneck in, 40–44, *41, 42, 43*; eliminating activities, 42, 55; rearranging activities, 44, 55, 55n1; shortening activities, 42–44, 55

Huddles: agenda items, 107–8; multidisciplinary rounds and, 113–14; resource coordination and, 107

ICU. *See* Intensive care unit

Identify the bottleneck (first focusing step), 11, 13, 15–23; case study, 20, *21,* 22; confirming your bottleneck, 19–20; emergency department, 17; inpatient units, 17–18; intensive care unit, 18–19; overview, 15–16; process map, creating, 19, 23; waiting room, 16

Identify the system's constraint (step 1), 71, 72–73; gaining momentum and, 125–26; to improve emergency department flow, 88–89; inpatient flow management and, 108

Idle time on bottleneck: minimizing or eliminating, 25–26, 33, 37, 39, 53

I Love Lucy (television show): Drum Buffer Rope illustration, 79–80

Imaging equipment: as constraint in imaging center, 132n1

Inertia: as new bottleneck, 66–67, 68; overcoming, 65, 68. *See also* Changed constraints / do not let inertia become the new system constraint

Infant mortality rate: in United States, 117

Inpatient beds: adding capacity to, 58–60; as a bottleneck resource, 30–32, 40–41, *41*; as a constraint, 108, 114–15, 116; productivity of, 108–9; reducing demand for, 60–61

Inpatient units: Buffer Management used in, 110–13; identifying bottlenecks in, 17–18; teamwork in, 107

Institute of Medicine, xix

Intensive care unit (ICU): identifying bottlenecks in, 18–19

International Ladies' Garment Workers' Union, 119

Interruptions: daily log of, maintaining, 130; minimizing, 129

Inventory, 73; biggest pileup of, looking for, 15, 22; decreasing, 6, 8, 9; definition of, 4; drinking fountain example, 38; effect of a productive move on operational measurements, 5, *5*; in healthcare systems, 6, 13; in hospital settings, 6; in Mattel factory example, 5, 6; staffing cuts and, 36–37; in Theory of Constraints, 4, *4. See also* Works-in-process

Isn't It Obvious? (Goldratt), 161

It's Not Luck (Goldratt), 161

Jacob, Dee, 162

Johnson, Lyndon B., 119

Joint Commission: patient flow standard of, xx

Toyota Way, The (Liker), 161
Triage: nurse-initiated order sets and, 97, 99
Turnover, 66

United States: healthcare expenditures in, 117
Urgent care centers/clinics, 62, 67, 121

Value Stream Mapping (VSM), 83–85, 84, 86, 103; definition of, 83; emergency department flow and application of, 90, 99, 100, 104; emergency department physician workflow, 90, 91, 92, 92; at Mattel factory, 84, 84–85; "pull till full" argument and, 96
Velocity (Jacob, Bergland, and Cox), 162
Volume: growing, 156
VSM. See Value Stream Mapping

Wadhwa, Gary, 161
Waiting room: identifying bottleneck in, 16
Wait times: average, 118; resource coordination and, 123
Works-in-process, 5; in dorm move-in example, 135; minimizing, 75. See also Inventory

About the Authors

Christopher Strear, MD, FACEP, earned a bachelor's degree in chemistry and English from Williams College and a medical degree from the University of Pennsylvania. He completed his residency training in emergency medicine at Harbor-UCLA Medical Center in Torrance, California, and is a Fellow of the American College of Emergency Physicians (ACEP). Dr. Strear is currently the director of patient flow, as well as director of revenue cycle management, for Northwest Acute Care Specialists and is an attending emergency physician at a Level 1 trauma center in Portland, Oregon. He is a member of the board of directors and the president-elect of the Oregon chapter of ACEP, and he serves on the ACEP National Reimbursement Committee. In addition, Dr. Strear is a clinical assistant professor of emergency medicine at Oregon Health and Sciences University in Portland.

Dr. Strear began his career in operational flow and process improvement as the director of patient flow at Legacy Emanuel Health Center in 2008. He published the first report in North America on hospital flow improvement using the Theory of Constraints ("Applying the Theory of Constraints to Emergency Department Workflow: Reducing Ambulance Diversion Through Basic Business Practice" in *Annals of Emergency Medicine*). His flow team has been twice awarded the John G. King Quality Award for accomplishments in clinical quality and process improvement. Dr. Strear has written many articles and book chapters. He has presented his research nationally and has lectured at hospitals and universities on patient flow. He is currently patient flow adviser and internal consultant to multiple hospital flow steering committees in the Pacific Northwest.

Danilo Sirias, PhD, earned a master's degree in industrial and systems engineering and a PhD in business administration, both from the University of Memphis. He is a Certified Critical Chain Project Manager and a certified Theory of Constraints International Certification Organization thinking process implementer. Dr. Sirias is currently a professor in the Department of Management and Marketing at Saginaw Valley State University.

Dr. Sirias is a coauthor of the book *Bridging the Boomer Xer Gap*, selected by Soundview Executive Summaries as one of the most influential business books of 2002 and by *ForeWord* magazine as Book of the Year. He has published peer-reviewed research in several journals, including the *Journal for Quality and Participation, International Journal of Applied Quality Management, International Journal of Production and Operation Management, International Journal of Production Research,* and *Journal of Education for Business.* Dr. Sirias has received multiple grants to further his research in the applications of the Theory of Constraints in healthcare. Dr. Sirias's research interests include managing patient flow in healthcare systems and developing strategies to improve quantitative reasoning. He is coauthor of the book *Success . . . an Adventure,* written to teach thinking strategies to teenagers. His latest book is *Problem Solving Maps,* a workbook designed to teach critical thinking skills through learning mathematics. His strategies for teaching math are used in several countries around the world.